UNIVERSITY OF MINNESOTA
THE INSTITUTE OF CHILD WELFARE
MONOGRAPH SERIES No. 1

THE YOUNG CHILD AND HIS PARENTS

A STUDY OF ONE HUNDRED CASES

BY

JOSEPHINE C. FOSTER, PH.D.
Assistant Professor, Institute of Child Welfare

AND

JOHN E. ANDERSON, PH.D.
Director, Institute of Child Welfare

GREENWOOD PRESS, PUBLISHERS
WESTPORT, CONNECTICUT

Library of Congress Cataloging in Publication Data

Foster, Josephine Curtis, 1889-1941.
  The young child and his parents.

    Reprint of the 1927 ed. published by the University of
Minnesota Press, Minneapolis, which was issued as
no. 1 of Monograph series of the Institute of Child
Welfare, University of Minnesota.
    Includes index.
    1. Child study. 2. Children in the United States--
Case studies. I. Anderson, John Edward, 1893-1966,
joint author. II. Title. III. Series: Minnesota.
University. Institute of Child Development and Welfare.
Monograph series ; no. 1.
HQ772.F64 1975   155.4   73-141546
ISBN 0-8371-5893-1

Originally published in 1927 by The University of Minnesota
Press, Minneapolis

Reprinted with the permission of The University of Minnesota
Press

Reprinted in 1975 by Greenwood Press,
a division of Williamhouse-Regency Inc.

Library of Congress Catalog Card Number 73-141546

ISBN 0-8371-5893-1

Printed in the United States of America

PREFACE

In the following pages there will be found one hundred brief case histories describing behavior shown by children between the ages of two and six. The upper limit was placed at six years in order to include all children not yet in school. These histories should be of value to parents who, through the study of other children, may gain some insight into their own particular problems and to students of child behavior and teachers of child care and development who through the description of many cases may gain knowledge and understanding of the young child. To the general reader, such a collection may be of interest since the wealth of illustrative material gives a picture of the conduct of the young child under the influence of the home environment.

In presenting these cases, the Institute of Child Welfare of the University of Minnesota wishes to acknowledge the coöperation of the Minneapolis Child Guidance Clinic, the St. Paul Child Guidance Clinic, and the Infant Welfare Society of Minneapolis, organizations which have been generous in assisting in many ways. The Institute also expresses its indebtedness to Dr. Smiley Blanton, Dr. M. L. Stiffler, Dr. E. J. Huenekens, Dr. Edith Boyd, Dr. Grace Arthur, Dr. Florence L. Goodenough, Miss Helen Peck, Miss Edith D. Dixon, Mrs. Marion Faegre, Miss Margaret G. Wood, Miss Adelia Boynton, Miss Marjorie J. Walker, and Miss Catherine Thompson.

CONTENTS

PART I. INTRODUCTION

Purpose and Method

Within the last decade, there has developed in this country a tremendous interest in the young child, and in the much more neglected subject of training for parenthood. Approach has been made from a number of different points of view by a variety of research groups, behavior clinics, nursery schools, and groups of parents themselves. There has been an increasing recognition of the fact that the mere being a father or a mother is not in itself sufficient to prepare the individual for the complex and difficult task of rearing children.

The interest which originally concerned itself with the young child as an entity has developed into a study of the child in his home situation, that is, in relation to his parents. Improvement in the methods of handling young children depends in large part upon making accessible to parents the results of broad experience and scientific study of the child and in impressing parents with the importance of the part they themselves play. All parents are interested in their children, but not all parents are interested in an impersonal study of them and in a deliberate effort toward modification of their own relationships with their children.

The part played by parents in the development of the child is so evident when case histories are considered in detail that it has seemed worth while to present a considerable number of cases equably distributed over the pre-school period. Here parents will find themselves and their children in many different relationships and under many situations. Teachers will become acquainted with the early home life of their pupils, and the old bachelor will see all the irritating traits of his nieces and nephews.

Case studies of certain pre-school children have, of course, already been published. Woolley[1] has studied the histories of several children in detail. Thom[2] has presented a number of behavior problems, and there are other histories scattered through the literature. A shortcoming of all these, from the standpoint of parent education, lies in the fact that they tend to describe extreme deviations of behavior and conduct. In the older literature on the young child there are a number of biographical studies describing in minute detail the development of a few superior children. The very length and detail of these studies make them unwieldly for many practical purposes.

In the brief case histories which we present, the general environmental situation of the child is described together with the behavior or conduct problems developing in the home before the school age. Where possible, we have outlined the modification which has been introduced in the endeavor to improve the behavior of both parent and child. The histories have been obtained from interviews with parents, teachers, and other adults in close contact with the child. Realizing that the unusual and striking case is far easier to locate than the usual or ordinary case, an attempt has been made to counteract this tendency and to secure as representative a group of histories as was possible. To this end, we have interviewed the parents of many children whose behavior has never been discussed with a physician or welfare worker and who have not been in contact with any clinic or social agency. On the other hand, we have purposely eliminated cases which were so abnormal and unusual as to fall outside ordinary experience.

[1]Woolley, H. T., Personality Studies of Three-Year-Olds. Journ. Exp. Psych. V. (1922), pp. 381–391; David, Child Welfare League of America, Case Studies, No. 2; Agnes, Ped. Sem. and Journ. of Genetic Psych., XXXII, (1925), pp. 569–598; Peter, Ped. Sem. and Journ. of Genetic Psych., XXXIII, (1926), pp. 9–29.

[2]Thom, D. A., Habit Clinics for the Child of Pre-school Age, Children's Bureau (U. S. Department of Labor), Pub. No. 135.

In this respect, our collection differs from those previously published.

Although our original purpose in collecting the hundred cases presented hereafter was to study the normal young child and to gain some insight into the types of reaction which he shows, it became increasingly apparent as we proceeded that what we were studying was a series of home situations, in which the parents played a most important part. The young child is not a thing detached and apart from his home but is very much part and parcel of that environment. In a very real sense, he can be said to mirror the home situation. His difficulties, problems, and modes of response are not exclusively the product of his own nature but are also the result of the stimulation which he is receiving from his environment.

No one can read the cases presented in this monograph without having the conclusion forcibly driven home that the problem of correcting the child is not entirely a problem of changing the child's reaction but frequently involves the problem of educating the parent with reference to his handling of the situation. Instance after instance occurs in which the disinterested onlooker would recognize the difficulty as one due to a parental reaction of which the parent was perhaps unaware. Frequently the reader will long to correct the parent rather than the child.

Illustration will be found of the conscientious but nearsighted parent who loses sight of the future development of his offspring in his attempt to satisfy the convenience of the moment. Lack of consideration for this later development is found in very different types of parents. We see one mother constantly giving in to temper tantrums for the sake of temporary peace, when she is thereby building up a very undesirable emotional reaction that will cause all manner of trouble in later years. Another mother forces such immediate and implicit obedience that she stunts the originality and initiative which would be of great importance and value fifteen years later. It is obvious that the child is not merely a plaything for the parent nor a convenient errandboy but should be thought of as a future contributing member of the community. In many cases parents refuse to recognize the fact that their favorite method of control does not work. They seem unable to modify their attitude toward the child and instead of dropping their fruitless method, merely intensify their mode of reaction to the situation. When an attempt to eradicate a child's shyness by the use of mild sarcasm results in greater shyness, instead of changing the method, some parents become more caustic. Their reaction in this situation is somewhat similar to that of a person who meets a foreigner with only a smattering of English, and who in his attempt to make the individual understand, repeats the same words louder and louder thereby blurring the sounds and making recognition more difficult. If the individual would speak more clearly rather than more loudly, the foreigner would understand more readily. It is so with our handling of children. Many times, we figuratively speak louder when we should be speaking more clearly to the child; we intensify our original method instead of trying a different mode of attack. The causes of human behavior are so complex and so involved that no single method or single procedure can dogmatically be said to meet a particular situation. The reader of these pages will be impressed with the variety of methods used by parents in different situations and with the fact that one method seems to be successful in one situation and unsuccessful in another similar situation. Effective handling of the child depends in part upon an experimental attitude toward him, a willingness to try one method until it has been clearly proven a failure, plus a readiness to shift to another method quickly when the first has proved unsuccessful.

Another mode of procedure which appears again and again is that of parents who in attempting to stop a bad habit by some type of punishment or disapproval succeed only in fixating the attention of children upon the habit. The child then goes through the undesirable behavior more often than was previously the case, a result exactly the opposite of that sought by the parent.

The far reaching effects of partiality in the family situation are shown clearly. On the one hand parents may fail to recognize differences in the ability of children and differences in their ages and so fail to make adequate provision for such differences. On the other hand, parents may over-emphasize and exaggerate minor differences of little significance. The behavior of the mother upon the arrival of a new baby is a frequent basis for jealousy. Engrossed with the care of the new child, she necessarily gives him a great deal of the time and attention previously bestowed upon the older child. She unconsciously expects the older child, wholly unprepared for the new situation, to act toward the new baby much as she herself does and is somewhat irritated at his suddenly exaggerated demands upon her attention. To the older child, however, the baby is a usurper and the mother's behavior is partiality. Still more serious in its emotional effects upon the child is the situation if further experience confirms his suspicions that the parent really prefers the other child. On the other hand, injustice is also done to a child when his parents assume him to be the mental duplicate of an actually superior child and try to make him live up to their estimate.

Not only is the child affected by the direct relationship to each parent but he is also to a surprising degree affected by the relationship between the parents themselves. Again and again there appear in these pages the recurring weakening of parental control by open argument about discipline in the presence of the child. Sometimes this takes the form of discussion as to whether the child should be punished or not, at other times of discussion as to the manner of punishment, and at still other times of argument after punishment has been given. Further, one parent frequently actually interferes with the carrying out of the directions of the other. In some families, relatives or other adults play a similar part in confusing the child and weakening discipline at its source. In a number of cases, in which this factor does not appear directly, it can be read between the lines.

Although many times the child is personally concerned with the topic of argument, he is emotionally disturbed also by any heated argument or difference between adults. Some parents have been amazed at seeing their child burst into tears during a friendly and jocular spat at breakfast in which there was no feeling. The child, in such cases, mistakes apparent enmity for real enmity. How much more disturbing is the situation where parents are in deadly earnest and emotionally aroused! Acknowledged incompatibility between parents subjects the child to a continuous emotional conflict which many times accounts for his later unstable conduct.

In reading the cases through, one is impressed with the frequency with which nervousness of the mother appears in connection with behavior problems in the child. The term "nervousness" as used is not to be interpreted as pathological nervousness, but rather as the statement the mother has made with reference to herself or as the statement made by an interviewer. In other words, the term "nervousness" is used in its popular sense. Some of the mothers so described are undoubtedly nervous. Others are merely using the term as an excuse for their own failure with the child. That a mother calls herself nervous is, however, significant, for it probably means that she suspects she could use greater self-control if she tried. She either fails to recognize the importance of such control or knows no method by which it could be acquired.

That a lack of balance, of common sense and of a feeling for the relative importance of various experiences in the life of the child is present in the homes of many problem children becomes apparent to even the most casual reader. Some parents place so much emphasis upon small and insignificant details, such as the proper greeting of a stranger, that they lose sight of more fundamental adjustments, such as the technique of getting along with other children. Some parents dote so upon their child that they give in to him on all occasions. Other parents are so rigorous and strict that the child feels they have no affection for him and so fails to build up a sound and wholesome emotional life. Some parents are in such constant contact with their child that he fails to develop self-reliance and the ability to play happily with other children. Other parents are so little in contact with their families that the children are deprived of valuable intellectual, social, and moral stimulation. A procedure of great value used in moderation and on the appropriate occasion may, carried to excess, be fraught with danger for the all-round development of the child.

We hoped at one time to summarize the parental aspects of these cases and prepare statistical tables similar to those which appear later for the children's characteristics. We regret that this has been impossible because cases collected primarily from the point of view of the child exhibit so many gaps in the parental data. Doubtless the reader will form many impressions which will give him a general notion of the results obtainable from a study definitely planned to deal with the family and the home.

In the following section will be found a statistical summary which includes studies of the cases by sex, chronological age, mental age, occupational class of parents, and type of problem.

In Part II will be found one hundred case histories arranged in order of chronological age from the youngest at two years to the oldest at six years and eleven months. In the presentation of these cases we are not advocating any particular method of treating young children nor attempting to substantiate any theory either of cause or treatment. Whether different results are due to differences in method used, in the children, in the parents, in the general situations in which the children were placed, or to the re-education of the parents by the physician and social worker is not always evident. We are simply presenting the histories as they were obtained, stripped of interpretation and of unessentials.

At the beginning of each history there is a brief characterization of the salient features of the case. In the history itself a uniform plan has been followed: first, a brief description of the home situation; second, a discussion of the developmental history; third, a history of the adjustments of the child; fourth, where possible, the treatment which was suggested; and fifth, the later history. In giving the treatment suggested for a particular case, we have tried to select the essential points rather than to report the detailed recommendations. As a matter of fact, the specific remedies suggested were frequently unimportant in comparison with the gradual re-education of the parents undertaken by the physician in his successive interviews. To the student and reader, the trend of this re-education will be evident on reading the entire history although no specific statements may be made in the suggested treatment that would indicate the line of attack.

At the end of the case histories, there will be found a rather detailed index. The entries in this index cover the separate problems mentioned throughout the case histories, the names of the children, and striking points in the individual histories. Reference is both to case number and to page. The index may be used to locate all cases showing a particular problem or to find some one particular case where the name of the child or a striking characteristic of the case is remembered.

STATISTICAL SUMMARY BASED ON 118 CASES

Various aspects of the histories are summarized in this section to give a general view of the cases as a whole. In order to understand their significance, the manner in which the cases were collected should be kept in mind.

From a large number of case histories obtained from various sources, we first discarded most of the obviously feeble-minded children, since the proportion of these reaching clinics and institutions is much larger than the proportion in the general population. Next, we discarded those cases in which the behavior difficulty was connected with a very unusual physical condition, such as a presumably still active sleeping sickness or a strikingly early sex maturity. Next, we eliminated histories which were, for some reason or other, so unusual that the identity of the child could not be readily concealed. Finally, histories which so nearly duplicated cases already obtained that they added little to the collection were dropped. This process of selection reduced the number of cases to be studied in detail to one hundred and eighteen. From these we selected the one hundred histories which seemed to us to be of the most general interest for publication in this report. The eighteen cases discarded were evenly scattered as to sex, chronological age, and problem, and added nothing new to the one hundred finally selected. *All tables, however, were based on the one hundred and eighteen cases.*

In reading the case histories and statistical summary, the reader will of course keep clearly in mind the limitations imposed by the method thru which the material was selected. The main part of the histories was of necessity secured from the parents. Since parents vary widely in intelligence, education, insight, and emotional attitude toward their children, their reports will vary similarly in accuracy, completeness, understanding and emphasis on particular items. Further, reports may be colored by the interest, indifference, or anxiety of the parents and by the personal and emotional relations which exist between the parent and the child.

Moreover, behavior which is quite normal may be characterized as of the problem variety by some parents. Parents of small children, on account of lack of experience with considerable numbers of children, have no criteria against which to weigh their own child's behavior. On the other hand, there are parents who because of indifference or an easy-going attitude, overlook or treat as of small moment extreme deviations of conduct and accept their child's behavior as natural and commonplace.

The parents' point of view also changes with the age of the child. A mother's description of the conduct of her two year old child will include some details which would not be included if the same mother were describing the conduct of the child at the age of six. The histories of older children doubtless omit some problems which were conspicuous at an early age, while the histories of the younger children may over-emphasize problems which are very temporary. In some of the cases, this difficulty is obviated since the history was taken at intervals over several years.

A collection of case histories suffers also from what we may call the labelling error. What one person may term irritable behavior, another may term vindictive or obstinate behavior; what one person may consider a feeding problem, another may describe as an emotional difficulty. So complex are the foundations of our conduct and so involved are the inter-relations of particular acts that it is impossible for a single individual, however expert he may be, to classify the child's behavior with a high degree of consistency and accuracy. Histories are also colored to some extent by the interests of the interviewer securing the story, who may emphasize points in which she is particularly interested and may unintentionally slight other points. It is probable that in a collection of cases such as this some labelling errors may cancel each other. Furthermore, in the statistical summary of the cases in the following section, the grouping of similar problems together in tables and charts tends to reduce the extent of the error.

Because our cases have been selected with several criteria in mind and from a number of sources, the reader should be careful not to make too wide generalizations from the tables. Our interest has been not so much in the frequency of particular problems in the population at large, as in obtaining accounts of many different problems and methods of control. Table I shows how the cases are distributed by sex and by chronological age. In general, the cases are fairly evenly divided between the various chronological ages with slightly fewer younger and slightly more older children. Because of the age distribution, a reasonably representative picture of behavior at various levels may be gained. There are more boys than girls.

TABLE I

Distribution of all cases by sex and chronological age

Chronological age	Boys	Girls	Total
2 to 2½ yrs.	4	5	9
2½ to 3 yrs.	8	1	9
3 to 3½ yrs.	4	5	9
3½ to 4 yrs.	4	7	11
4 to 4½ yrs.	7	7	14
4½ to 5 yrs.	7	5	12
5 to 5½ yrs.	7	6	13
5½ to 6 yrs.	4	4	8
6 to 6½ yrs.	12	8	20
6½ to 7 yrs.	9	4	13
Totals	66	52	118

A distribution of all cases by sex and mental age[3] is given in Table II.

[3]For the benefit of readers not working in this field, the following explanation of mental age and intelligence quotients is appended. In stating that a child has a mental age of four years, we mean that he has the intellectual development of the average child of four as measured by an intelligence test. The mental age itself does not tell the whole story, since the same mental age may be obtained by children of widely different chronological ages. It is evident that a child with a chronological age of four and a mental age of four may be considered as having an average intellectual development, while a child of three with a mental age of four is ahead mentally, and the child of five with a mental age of four is retarded. By dividing the mental age by the chronological age, we may obtain a quotient, commonly called the Intelligence Quotient, or IQ, thus expressing in one number the relation of mental age to chronological age. For a child of four with a mental age of four, this would be 100,

It will be seen that the great majority of mental ages fall between three and six years with a small scattering of children running into the ages above seven years. In twenty of the cases, the mental ages had not been determined.

TABLE II

Distribution of all cases by sex and mental age

Mental age	Boys	Girls	Total
2	0	2	2
3	7	5	12
4	11	10	21
5	17	15	32
6	9	9	18
7	6	3	9
8	1	2	3
9	0	1	1
Undetermined	15	5	20

The distribution of all cases by intelligence quotients[3] given in Table III shows that the great majority of our children lie between 80 and 130 IQ with the mean at 110. This is not to be interpreted as showing a superior group, since other investigations on unselected children in the pre-school period seem to show that the scales now in use for this period rate children in general somewhat too high.

TABLE III

Distribution of all cases by sex and intelligence quotient

Intelligence Quotient	Boys no. of cases	Girls no. of cases	Totals no. of cases	Percentage
50 to 59	0	1	1	1.0
60 to 69	1	0	1	1.0
70 to 79	2	0	2	2.0
80 to 89	7	6	13	13.3
90 to 99	8	6	14	14.3
100 to 109	8	3	11	11.2
110 to 119	10	13	23	23.5
120 to 129	9	10	19	19.4
130 to 139	3	4	7	7.1
140 to 149	3	4	7	7.1

for a child of three with a mental age of four, it would be 133, and for a child of five with a mental age of four, 80. Other things being equal, children with IQ's below 70 are considered very inferior. from 70–90, inferior, from 90–110, average, 110–130, superior, and above 130, very superior.

TABLE IV

Distribution of all cases by father's occupational class

Occupational class	no. of cases	Percentage of cases	Percentage in the total population
Professional	26	24.5	5.4
Semi-professional and managerial	15	14.2	6.4
Highly skilled trades and clerical	33	31.1	36.6
Less skilled trades and minor clerical	15	14.2	24.4
Semi- and slightly skilled	11	10.4	14.9
Unskilled labor	6	5.7	12.0
Unknown	12		

In Table IV we have made a study of the distribution of cases by the father's occupational class, using as a basis of comparison the 14th census of the United States.[4] The various occupations listed for the city of Minneapolis have been divided into six categories in accordance with the Barr scale for occupational intelligence and the Taussig industrial classification, descriptions of which may be found in "Genetic Studies of Genius."[5] We have calculated the percentages of males between the ages of twenty-one and forty-five years engaged in each of these types of occupations, and listed the resulting figures in the third column of Table IV. In this table, then, there is given in the first column the number of cases in each class for our group; in the second, the percentage of these cases and in the third, the percentage of the occupations found in the total population of Minneapolis based upon the census figures. It will be seen that in our collection there are a larger percentage of individuals in classes I and II, the professional and semi-professional and managerial classes, and smaller percentages in the semi-skilled and unskilled labor classes. This is not to be interpreted as indicating that behavior problems are more likely to arise in children whose fathers are grouped in classes I and II, but rather as an indication of the fact that individuals in these classes are much more likely to take advantage of the opportunities offered by children's clinics and research organi-

[4]For 1920, Volume IV, Table 2, pages 1144–1146
[5]Terman *et al.*, Stanford University Press. 1925, pages 66–72

zations. A sampling error in the selection of the group rather than any characteristic of the children increases the percentage in the upper classes. In any event, the group of cases contains representatives from all the occupational classes found in a typical city in proportions not greatly different from those found in the total population. While they cannot be said exactly to represent a cross-section of children in the community nevertheless they probably approximate this as nearly as any to be found in the literature now.

TABLE V

Classification of all cases by problem and sex

Problem	Number of cases			Percentage of cases		
	Boys	Girls	Total	Boys	Girls	Total
Fears	13	14	27	19.7	26.9	22.9
Temper tantrums ...	12	6	18	18.2	11.5	15.3
Other emotions	23	21	44	34.8	40.4	37.3
Nervous habits[6]	21	13	34	31.8	25.0	28.8
Over-dependent	5	2	7	7.6	3.8	5.9
Hyper-active	9	7	16	13.6	13.5	13.6
Fatigue	10	2	12	15.2	3.8	10.2
Sleeping	7	10	17	10.6	19.2	14.4
Handling genitals . ..	2	4	6	3.0	7.7	5.1
Toilet habits	7	5	12	10.6	9.6	10.2
Feeding	18	18	36	27.3	34.6	30.5
Over-imaginative . ..	3	4	7	4.5	7.7	5.9
Improper language ..	4	1	5	6.1	1.9	4.2
Speech	13	8	21	19.7	15.4	17.8
Playmates	12	7	19	18.2	13.5	16.1
Authority	21	14	35	31.8	26.9	29.7
School	11	0	11	16.7	0.0	9.4
Miscellaneous[7]	11	8	19	16.7	15.4	16.1
Total number of problems shown	202	144	346			
Number of cases	66	52	118			
Average number of problems per case	3.1	2.8	2.9			

[6]The group of "nervous habits" includes: thumb-sucking, boy, 2 yr. 1 mo.; boy, 2 yr. 9 mo.; boy, 2 yr. 11 mo.; girl, 4 yr. 3 mo.; girl, 4 yr. 4 mo.; girl, 4 yr. 10 mo.; boy, 5 yr. 0 mo.; girl, 5 yr. 1 mo.; boy, 5 yr. 11 mo.; boy 6 yr. 11 mo.; finger sucking, girl, 2 yr. 10 mo.; girl. 4 yr. 2 mo.; girl, 4 yr. 5 mo.; girl 6 yr. 3 mo.; nail biting, girl, 2 yr. 2 mo.; boy, 2 yr. 10 mo.; boy, 3 yr. 0 mo.; boy, 4 yr. 1 mo.; boy, 4 yr. 6 mo.; girl, 6 yr. 3 mo.;

A distribution by type of problem and sex in terms both of number of cases and percentage is given in Table V. The percentage figures are obtained by dividing the frequency of the given problem by the total number of boys, girls, or both combined as the case may be. In studying these percentages the reader should remember that one child may present several different types of problem.

In spite of the difficulties inherent in a classification by problem we have attempted to group our cases sufficiently to bring out salient features. "Fears" includes also timidity and night terrors. "Temper tantrums" includes all kinds from major tantrums in which the child throws himself about on the floor to minor ones in which he stands still and screams in an uncontrolled manner. "Other emotional problems" includes types of behavior described as antagonism, daydreaming, destructiveness, excitability, feeling of inferiority, indifference, impulsiveness, extreme inhibition, irritability, jealousy, repression, self-consciousness, selfishness, sensitiveness, shyness, showing off, "spoiled," unhappiness, emotional instability, instability of attention, and vindictiveness. The various items under "nervous habits" have already been listed in foot-note 6. "Overdependent" means over-dependence on one or both parents. "Sleeping" includes problems connected with naps as well as the night sleep. "Over-imaginative" includes lying. "Improper

nervous, girl, 2 yr. 0 mo.; girl, 2 yr. 2 mo.; girl, 3 yr. 8 mo.; girl, 4 yr. 6 mo.; boy, 5 yr. 11 mo.; boy, 6 yr. 1 mo.; boy, 6 yr. 5 mo.; boy, 6 yr. 5 mo.; boy, 6 yr. 9 mo.; twitches, boy, 6 yr. 5 mo.; boy, 6 yr. 6 mo.; fidgety, boy, 6 yr. 11 mo.; tic, boy, 5 yr. 2 mo.

[7]Under miscellaneous there are grouped a considerable number of problems which occur so infrequently as not to justify inclusion in the main table. They are as follows: periodic vomiting, boy, 5 yr. 2 mo.; screams when touched, boy 2 yr. 2 mo.; feminine characteristics in a boy, 6 yr. 10 mo.; objects to having curls brushed, girl, 4 yr. 6 mo.; eats mud, girl, 4 yr. 5 mo.; runs away, girl, 4 yr. 5 mo.; girl, 6 yr. 5 mo.; slow in dressing, girl, 4 yr. 5 mo.; boy, 4 yr. 9 mo.; unusual pains, girl 3 yr. 2 mo.; chews hair, girl, 4 yr. 10 mo.; slow in learning certain habits, boy, 4 yr. 9 mo.; starts fires, boy, 6 yr. 10 mo.; poor motor control, girl, 4 yr. 1 mo.; boy, 6 yr. 4 mo.; listless, girl, 5 yr. 1 mo.; boy, 6 yr. 11 mo.; meticulous, boy, 3 yr. 4 mo.; boy, 5 yr. 0 mo.; petty stealing, girl, 6 yr. 5 mo.; boy, 6 yr. 11 mo.

language" includes swearing and language said to be "shocking." "Speech" includes baby-talk, lisping, stuttering, and so on. "Playmates" includes such things as annoying other children, bullying, cruelty to others, quarrelsomeness and teasing. "Authority" signifies a poor attitude toward authority and includes disobedience, impudence, obstinacy, negativism, and a stoical attitude in punishment. The points listed under "Miscellaneous" have already been given in foot-note 7.

It is apparent from Table V that certain types of problem are much more frequent than are other types. Emotional adjustments, including fears and temper tantrums, offer by far the greatest number of problems. Nervous habits, feeding problems and conflicts with authority also occur in more than one quarter of the cases, whereas over-dependence, handling genitals, over-imaginative behavior, improper language and school difficulties are found in less than one tenth of the cases.

If we consider the relationship of problem to sex, we find that on the average boys show slightly more problems than do girls; the boys have a mean of 3.1, while the girls have a mean of 2.8 problems. This seems to be primarily due to the fact that the boys show temper tantrums, fatigue, improper language, and school difficulties more frequently than do girls. The remaining percentages show small differences or else are based on too few cases to justify comparisons between the sexes. A possible exception may be sleeping problems, which are somewhat more frequent among girls than boys.

A classification of all cases by problems and chronological age may be found in Table VI. There is a general tendency for number of problems to increase with age; two-year olds showing an average of 1.8, three-year olds 2.5, four-year olds 3.5, five-year olds 3.0, and six-year olds 3.3 problems per case. Problems seem to reach their maximum frequency at four years and then either decrease or remain constant. It is possible that the decrease in behavior problems at five years of age arises out of the fact that many children then enter kindergarten and their objectionable conduct at home becomes less noticeable.

In Plate I, based upon Table VI we present in graphic form some of the most striking relationships between age and frequency of problem. Fears are relatively infrequent at two years, reach their maximum at three years, occurring then in forty-five percent of the cases, diminish at four and five years, and diminish still further at six years. Temper tantrums show the maximum frequency at two years, are less frequent at ages three and four, and drop off still further at five years, Emotional problems other than fears and temper tantrums seem to increase with age, being relatively infrequent at two years, more frequent at three, and occurring in approximately half the cases at four, five, and six years. The nervous habits

TABLE VI

Classification of all cases by chronological age and problem

Problem	Number of cases at ages					Percentage of cases at ages				
	2	3	4	5	6	2	3	4	5	6
Fears	3	9	5	6	4	16.7	45.0	19.3	28.6	12.1
Temper tantrums	5	3	4	2	4	27.8	15.0	15.4	9.5	12.1
Other emotions	1	4	12	9	18	5.5	20.0	46.2	42.9	54.5
Nervous habits	6	3	7	7	11	33.3	15.0	26.9	33.3	33.3
Over-dependent	1	1	3	1	1	5.5	5.0	11.5	4.8	3.0
Hyper-active	0	0	6	5	5	0.0	0.0	23.1	23.8	15.1
Fatigue	0	2	1	6	3	0.0	10.0	3.8	28.6	9.1
Sleeping	2·	6	4	1	4	11.1	30.0	15.4	4.8	12.1
Handling genitals	2	1	1	0	2	11.1	5.0	3.8	0.0	6.1
Toilet problems	1	2	3	2	4	5.5	10.0	11.5	9.5	12.1
Feeding	1	9	11	6	9	5.5	45.0	42.3	28.6	27.3
Over-imaginative	0	0	4	0	3	0.0	0.0	15.4	0.0	9.1
Improper language	0	0	1	1	3	0.0	0.0	3.8	4.8	9.1
Speech	5	2	7	3	4	27.8	10.0	26.9	14.3	12.1
Playmates	2	2	8	3	4	11.1	10.0	30.8	14.3	12.1
Authority	3	4	10	7	11	16.7	20.0	38.5	33.3	33.3
School	0	0	0	2	9	0.0	0.0	0.0	9.5	27.3
Miscellaneous	1	2	5	2	9	5.5	10.0	19.2	9.5	27.3
Number of cases	18	20	26	21	33					
Average number of problems per age ..	1.8	2.5	3.5	3.0	3.3					

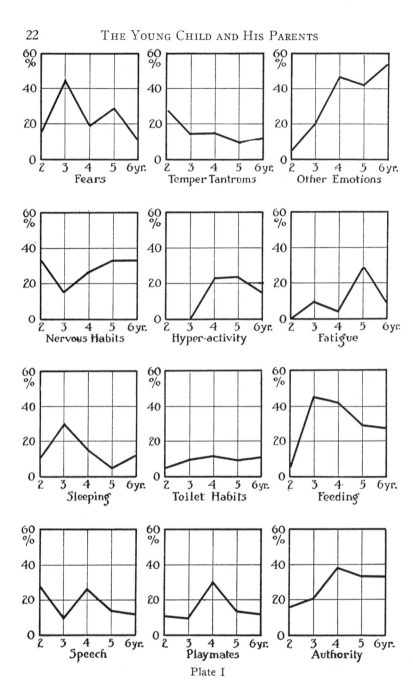

Plate I

are fairly constant throughout the whole age range, with an unexplained drop at three. Hyper-activity seems to be taken as a matter of course in the two and three year olds, becomes a problem at four, and diminishes at six years. Fatigue as a problem reaches its maximum in the five year olds. Difficulties in sleeping are most frequent among three year old children, possibly because some children at this age begin to object to naps. Problems centering about toilet habits are relatively constant at all ages. Feeding problems are at their maximum among three and four year old children, diminishing quite decidedly among five and six year olds. There is a minimum at two years of age, probably because up to this age many children are still fed by their parents. Speech difficulties show some tendency to decrease with age. Difficulties with playmates are not of great importance except at four years. Before this age it has not been necessary for the child to make social adjustments and after this age they have found out how to get along with others or, in the case of kindergarten children, make contacts under supervision. Unfavorable reactions to authority increase from two to four years and then remain constant to six years. The miscellaneous problems cover such a wide variety of reactions that no comparison on the basis of age is justified.

In summarizing our findings, the following points may be noted:

1. Our cases are fairly equally divided between the different chronological ages and the sexes.

2. The great majority of the children have mental ages between three and six years.

3. The distribution of intelligence is slightly skewed toward the upper levels.

4. A distribution of cases by father's occupational class approximates that of the total population with a tendency for a larger percentage in the professional and semi-professional

classes and with a lower percentage in the less skilled and un-skilled classes.

5.   A classification of cases by problem and sex shows a slightly greater number of problems in boys than girls, with no very marked differences for the individual problems.

6.   A classification of the cases by problem and age shows a tendency for problems to increase somewhat with age. A detailed study shows variation in the frequency of the separate problems at the different ages.

PART II. ONE HUNDRED CASE HISTORIES

In the following pages there are presented one hundred cases of young children between the ages of two and six years, arranged in order of chronological age. Occasionally two children in the same family are described, in which event many details are so much alike that the two are written up together and will be found at the age of the younger child, with a cross reference included at the age of the older child.

Cases exhibiting any particular behavior trait may be located through the index. A variety of methods have been used to conceal the identity of the individual children, such as a change in name and in the unessential features of the case history.

CASE 1. GLADYS HIGGINS   TWO YEARS AND NO MONTHS
Nervousness. Fears.

Home Situation.—Both Mr. and Mrs. Higgins are even tempered people, happy and congenial. Mr. Higgins is a telegraph operator with eighth grade education; his wife graduated from high school. The presence of the maternal grandfather in no way interferes with the harmony of the household. In fact, when Mrs. Higgins is ill, he cares for Gladys, the only child.

Developmental History.—Gladys had spasms of the stomach at birth and was kept in the hospital for the first three months of her life. She walked at one year and talked very early. She has had none of the children's diseases and is in excellent physical condition. She has an IQ of 126.[1]

History of Adjustments.—Although Gladys has not yet acquired perfect bladder control, she will keep dry for three or four days in succession. She has always been considered extremely "nervous." She develops fears suddenly without apparent cause. She is afraid of the vacuum cleaner, of large dogs, and of the

[1] See footnote 3 page 13.

dark. She goes to the window and cries about the dark though she is not afraid to go to sleep in a dark room with the door almost closed. This fear may possibly be based on an overheard remark that a little friend "must go home as it's getting dark." The fear of dogs seemed to be transferred to an unfamiliar object when the child was taken to visit a friend. As Gladys entered the front hall she began to scream that she was "afraid of wow-wow.' There was no dog in the house and the object of her fear apparently was a sewing cabinet. On her next visit she was taken in by the back door and the sewing cabinet had been moved from its place. The child looked for it but did not scream when she saw it in the new corner.

Mrs. Higgins seems to use wisdom in handling Gladys. She tries to avoid situations or conversation that may arouse fear. She also recognizes that the child is too much with adults and tries to remedy this by taking her to parks to play with other children and to visit friends who have children. Gladys occasionally plays with some very rough children in the neighborhood but more frequently with a girl a year older than herself.

CASE 2. WALTER THAYER   Two YEARS AND Two MONTHS
    Spoiled. Restless sleep. Screams when touched. Scalp disease.

Home Situation.—Walter's father is a janitor and the family live in a small house which is fairly well furnished and very neat and clean. They mix little with their neighbors, partly because Mr. Thayer is such a quiet man and partly because Mrs. Thayer is completely wrapped up in her home. Neither parent appears to be particularly intelligent. All the members of the family think everything Walter does is "cute" and they spoil him consistently. Although Mrs. Thayer frequently tells him what to do, she is satisfied with thinking that he "minds pretty well for a small child." The other children, to whom she is almost equally devoted, are sisters of nineteen and eighteen, a brother of fifteen, a brother of eleven who is in a special class at school and another brother of five.

Developmental History.—Walter was not a fussy baby. He began to walk at eleven months. His mother cannot remember when he began talking, but he is talking well at present. He has had no contagious diseases. At the present time he shows average development and nourishment, large and red tonsils, and a scalp disease. He refused to cooperate well enough for the psychologist to obtain a mental rating, but he answered a sufficient number of questions to persuade the examiner that he was at least of average intelligence.

History of Adjustments.—Walter is not capricious about his food though he eats principally eggs and toast and is not particularly fond of milk. Until two months ago he showed no problems whatever. He was a bit spoiled but had no nervous or undesirable habits. At that time, however, he changed from an alert, active, friendly child to one who screams whenever anyone touches or approaches him. He is now a very restless sleeper, thrashing around and throwing the covers off.

Suggested Treatment.—The clinic physician prescribed for the scalp condition and recommended that the boy be washed in olive oil instead of water. Mrs. Thayer was advised to stop treating the boy like a baby.

Later History.—Three months later Walter's scalp disease has cleared up. He is still somewhat shy but no longer screams when touched. His mother says he is now sleeping quietly.

CASE 3. ROSIE RILEY   Two YEARS AND Two MONTHS
Nervous. Spoiled. Nailbiting. Feeding problem.

Home Situation.—Rosie is an only child of parents in comfortable circumstances. They live in a well furnished house in a good neighborhood. Mr. and Mrs. Riley are devoted to the child and are perhaps overanxious to keep her happy. They are confident that she will outgrow her undesirable habits.

Developmental History.—Rosie was a colicky baby but otherwise gave her parents little concern. She had mumps before she was two years old and she has had many colds. Her tonsils were removed six weeks ago. In the clinic examination she was found to be well nourished but afflicted with worms. Rosie seems to be the intellectual equal of the average child of her age.

History of Adjustments.—Rosie has always had a poor appetite. She dislikes all kinds of food and complains of pain in her stomach when food is presented. She is ready, however, to eat between meals. She is a restless sleeper, bites her nails and according to Mrs. Riley is "nervous." She is also stubborn, easily angered, and "bossy" with other children. Her parents have taken Rosie to five or six doctors and clinics one after another and each time have been insulted when told that Rosie was a plain "spoiled child." They have then gone to others confident that some physician would find some physical cause for the "nervousness."

Suggested Treatment.—A physician should treat Rosie for the worms. Eating between meals should be stopped and the parents must be firmer in discipline. Mr. and Mrs. Riley should read Cameron's "Nervous Child."

Later History.—Two months later Mr. and Mrs. Riley report that they have entirely reversed their attitude. They have read Cameron through three times and are now convinced that they have been at fault in handling Rosie. They have changed their methods and when a few weeks ago Rosie started to stutter and later refused to talk, the parents remained unexcited and the child spoke naturally once more. Mr. and Mrs. Riley have made every effort to pay less attention to Rosie and to cease nagging at meal time. They have provided playmates for her and built her a play house. A year after the first interview the report is that Rosie has stopped her nailbiting, is eating much better, and is no longer a management problem. The recent arrival of a baby brother has helped draw attention away from Rosie and will probably improve the situation still more unless Rosie feels slighted and develops a jealousy.

CASES 4 AND 50. AGATHA DORSETT TWO YEARS AND THREE MONTHS
                 EDNA DORSETT   FOUR YEARS AND SEVEN MONTHS

Imaginative. Stubborn. Mild temper tantrums. Teasing.
Urges sister to naughtiness.

Home Conditions.—These children live in a well-furnished house in a good neighborhood. Their father has a responsible position in a public service corporation. He is a rather small man who is usually quiet and seldom raises his voice. At first acquaintance he seems a little over-indulgent, but he really has excellent control over his children. He gives few commands, but expects those few to be obeyed. He is also very careful to pay particular attention to Edna when her mother seems to be showing favoritism toward Agatha. Mrs. Dorsett is a very attractive woman, absorbed in her home and family, though not to the extent of abandoning outside social contacts. She is somewhat meticulous about the appearance of her house and children. Beside the two girls there is a baby boy, only a few weeks old.

Developmental History.—Edna was a frail, colicky baby for the first three months of her life. She is now tall, well developed and well nourished. She walked at sixteen months, spoke her first word at eleven months, and by the age of two was speaking with considerable facility. She had a light case of chicken-pox at the age of two. Soon after she was four she had her tonsils and adenoids removed. On the intelligence test she received an IQ of 120.

Agatha has always been a very healthy child. She was a good baby, walked at thirteen months, and talked before she was a year old. She is now a sturdy child with a "negative" report on her physical examination. She has had none of the contagious diseases. On the intelligence test she received an IQ of 120.

History of Adjustments.—With neither of these children have there been feeding, enuresis or sleeping problems. Both of them are still taking naps regularly every day. Edna seems to dream frequently, talks in her sleep often, and occasionally cries out. If she wakens and cries, she is taken to the toilet and afterwards sleeps quietly. She has never shown any special fears. She enjoys playing with dolls and blocks, but her favorite occupation is helping her mother about the house. She makes cocoa for her supper, usually makes her own bed, and her mother's bed as well, and so on. In good weather she spends practically the entire day out-of-doors. As a little baby she sucked her thumb, but this habit was outgrown without treatment or comment. She ate dirt and dirty snow till she was nearly two. At the age of eighteen months she ran into the street frequently. She was, at this time, allowed to go out alone but Mrs. Dorsett always watched from the porch or a window. Whenever the child ran into the street, her mother promptly administered a spanking and scolding. The parents were very consistent in teaching her to take their hands in crossing a street whenever they were out together, and by the age of two Edna had learned that when she was alone she must stay on her own side of the street. She has now learned to cross quickly after looking in both directions. Edna's chief problem at present is stubbornness. She stands still and screams when she cannot have her own way. She is particularly likely to be cross when she wakes from her nap. Mrs. Dorsett has tried several treatments for this. Spanking does absolutely no good, but ignoring and isolating her until she is agreeable seem to work fairly well. At other times Edna can be reasoned with, successfully. Edna recently has become so impressed with the advisability of telling the truth that she is convinced that she can do anything if she only tells about it afterward. Mrs. Dorsett is uncertain as to what the best method will be to gain not only general good behavior but also the truth about misdeeds. The only other definite problem which Edna shows is a decided tendency to tease other children, particularly those younger than herself. This results in spasms of anger in her sister Agatha.

Agatha is less of a problem than her sister. This may be because she is a very pretty, attractive child, flattered and caressed by all the neighbors and friends as well as by her parents. It seems probable that part of Edna's teasing may be traced to jealousy, for before the birth of Agatha, Edna was considered a "model child." Agatha obeys both her parents well and apparently does not need as tactful handling as Edna requires. She has never been punished severely, she is "too sweet." When she turns on the gas stove her hands are slapped hard enough to stop the activity for the time being, but not hard enough to have any lasting effect. She sleeps quietly and usually wakens once each night to be taken to the toilet.

As a baby Agatha sucked her thumb when going to sleep. This was cured by putting on mittens when the child was put to bed. She is now running into the street frequently, apparently for the fun of being pursued. If she is told to play in her own yard and left alone, she seldom ventures farther.

Agatha is very active and rather restless, seldom playing with any one thing for more than five minutes at a time. Most of the time she is with older children. She enters into their games readily and without interfering. She will occasionally "yell her head off" and scream till she is red in the face if she cannot have what she wants. Edna is fond of teasing Agatha and frequently snatches a toy from her, holds it out of reach and then laughs at Agatha's frantic struggles to recover it. Mrs. Dorsett intervenes at these times and tries to compromise, not letting either child have the advantage all of the time. Mrs. Dorsett is sometimes unable to tell whether Agatha's misdemeanors are of her own or of Edna's invention. She has occasionally heard Edna say to her sister "Go pull the table-cloth off, Agatha." The problem is how to punish each child, and how to discover the real culprit.

CASE 5.   ALICE WHITTIER   TWO YEARS AND THREE MONTHS
        Sleeping problem. Night terrors. Fear of bogie-man.

Home Situation.—Alice lives with her parents and baby sister in a well-furnished, home-like lower duplex in a rather poor neighborhood. Her father is a semi-skilled laborer, kind to his family, but with no particular force of character. Mrs. Whittier in spite of a pleasant, even-tempered disposition, has a sad, haunted expression. She tends to spoil the children. Her chief method of forcing obedience is to make threats about the "bogie-man."

Developmental History.—Alice was a fussy baby who was if anything a bit slow in gaining weight, walking and talking. She had measles at fifteen months but has in general been moderately well and is now fairly well developed and nourished.

History of Adjustments.—Alice is not a real feeding problem although her appetite is somewhat erratic. She occasionally exhibits a temper tantrum but is ordinarily easily managed. She still wets the bed each night and has always been a restless sleeper. Lately Alice has been having night terrors and has been waking up for the day at three or four o'clock in the morning. Since she sleeps in the room with her parents, this disturbs the entire family and Mrs. Whittier desires advice.

Suggested Treatment.—Alice should be given a warm bath at bed time to reduce her restlessness, her afternoon liquids should be restricted to aid in stopping the bed-wetting, she should be put in a room by herself when she wakens early, and above all she must no longer be terrified by tales of the bogie man.

Later History.—Two months later Mrs. Whittier reported good results of this treatment. Alice was then waking once in the night to go to the toilet, and never wetting the bed. She was sleeping more quietly and not waking so early in the morning. After another six months Alice began waking at four o'clock again, but her mother thought this was because relatives had spoiled her at Christmas. Mrs. Whittier immediately applied the measures that had been successful before with the result that Alice's regular sleeping hours were reestablished within a few days. At this point the family moved into a much better neighborhood where there were plenty of playmates. Alice's problems of restlessness and lack of appetite disappeared promptly, to reappear when a second move took the family into a childless block.

CASE 6. HERBERT ACH   TWO YEARS AND THREE MONTHS
Spoiled. Over-dependent on mother. Mean to other children.
Speech defect. Nervous mother.

Home Situation.—Herbert is an only child and lives with his parents in an upper duplex which is attractively furnished and moderately well kept. His father who is a truck driver seems to come in contact with Herbert but little. Mrs. Ach is nervous and highstrung and speaks very rapidly. She gives in to all her small son's whims. She has always been sorry he was not a girl.

Developmental History.—In early infancy Herbert had rickets, and was very irritable. He has had no major illnesses though his mother deliberately exposed him to whooping cough and chicken-pox. He has always been well, but has had a small appetite and is now definitely undernourished. He still wets the bed almost every night.

History of Adjustments.—Herbert has always been spoiled. He whines and cries and demands his mother's attention constantly. He cries when left in a room alone to play and that makes his mother "so nervous" that she plays with him. He refuses to go to bed till his mother does at 8:30. Other children refuse to play with him because he pinches and bites them.

Suggested Treatment and Results.—When Herbert was about two years old, Mrs. Ach took him to a clinic for advice. Their suggestions were: a reduction of liquids in the late afternoon to help the bed wetting; putting him to bed early and letting him cry till he got over the notion of sitting up with his mother; insisting that he play alone for a part of each day. Further suggestions that he be sent to an aunt for a visit were refused on the ground that Mrs. Ach would be "too lonesome without him." For two or three months after this Herbert's general behavior improved and Mrs. Ach lost some of her own nervousness. Then he was returned to the clinic with the report that the bed-wetting was still more frequent, he was mean to other children in the neighborhood, hard to manage, bold, selfish and "wild."

This time the physician advised firmer control and picking up during the night for the bed-wetting. Three months later Herbert's mother said the bed-wetting had become infrequent and that his general behavior was improved though at times he was very difficult. He now stutters considerably. His parents are enraged at this and think he does it "just to be mean." A month later Mrs. Ach reported that the physician's advice to stop punishing Herbert for stuttering had worked well, and he does it now only when over-tired. However, since Christmas he has been more difficult to manage than ever. Mrs. Ach was now told that she must let the child be away from her more and was advised to send him away for a visit. Herbert's mother seems nervously unstable and there seems little hope of getting the two separated. Whenever the physician gets the mother to agree to even a short separation, the grandmother and neighbors interfere and ask, "Aren't you his mother? and aren't you smart enough to bring up your own child?"

Since it seems impossible to separate mother and child even for a week, perhaps the most effective treatment would be to send Herbert, who is now four years old, to a private kindergarten where he will have to associate with other children and will be away from his mother part of each day.

CASE 7. EDITH McKAY   TWO YEARS AND FIVE MONTHS

Feeding problem. Not trained in toilet habits.
Refuses to nap anywhere except in baby buggy.

Home Situation.—The McKays seem to be a very happy family. The father is a mechanic in a garage and is a jolly man at home, devoted to his children. Mrs. McKay is lenient with the children and yet manages them well. She gives an impression of self-satisfaction which arouses a suspicion that suggestions, though pleasantly received, may not be tried out consistently. The other three children in the family are considerably older, a sister eighteen. a brother of sixteen, and a brother of nine. The home is a moderately well furnished house, neat and clean.

Developmental History.—Edith was an exceptionally good baby. She walked and talked at about a year. She has had no contagious diseases. She sleeps quietly. At present her general development is good and her nutrition fair.

History of Adjustments.—Edith has never had a good appetite and Mrs. McKay thinks her finicky notions about food may be copied from the older children in the family. Edith sometimes fails to obey and occasionally has a mild temper tantrum. She has not yet succeeded in establishing perfect bladder control, even in the daytime. Edith's speech is not plain, but is a mixture of German (spoken as a young girl by the mother) and English. She plays in the house all the time. Mrs. McKay's chief problem is that Edith refuses to take a nap or even to lie down in the afternoon in any place except her baby-carriage.

Suggested Treatment.—Edith must play outdoors some part of every day. Mrs. McKay should try restricting liquids in the late afternoon and taking the child up at night to prevent bedwetting. She should try isolating and ignoring for the tantrums and various schemes to persuade the child to take naps in her crib.

Later History.—A month later Edith's appetite, bed-wetting and temper tantrums are still about the same. She does eat when her mother says she can't go out to play till her plate is empty. Mrs. McKay is evidently not very firm. She says with so many children to feed and care for she has not time to make each one do just as she should. Edith is often not in bed before nine o'clock because the family go out together and take her along with them.

Five months later Mrs. McKay says that the isolating and ignoring treatments are working well on the tantrums. The bed-wetting is somewhat less frequent. Edith has recently acquired a mannerism of pulling one lock of her hair. She still insists on napping in the baby-buggy.

Six months later Mrs. McKay reports that Edith still refuses to nap in her crib even after she had become accustomed to napping in the same part of the room. The child is now so large that she is much cramped up in the buggy and her mother arranges things so that Edith's feet stick out of the end of the buggy onto the bed. Edith makes no objection when she wakens to find that her mother has moved her into the crib while she slept nor does she object to sleeping in her crib at night; but she consistently refuses to fall asleep in the afternoon anywhere but in the buggy.

CASE 8. FRANK FRENCH   TWO YEARS AND SIX MONTHS
   Restless sleeper. Exhausted mother. Unsympathetic father.

Home Situation.—The French family live in a small bungalow that is supplied with all the modern conveniences. Mr. French, who is a clerk in a large department store, is a stern man and the children respect him. He apparently realizes that his wife does not know how to manage the boys but he is unsympathetic and thinks her worn out condition is due to unnecessary worry. Mrs. French appears somewhat exhausted. Her discipline is very erratic; she spanks one moment and humors the next. A fourteen year old stepson seems to get along well in the home. He tries to help the mother in disciplining Frank and his three year old brother but he does not succeed very well and says that the two are "beginning to get on his nerves."

Developmental History.—Frank was a rather fussy baby, was very sensitive to colds and had measles when he was a year old. His physical examination at present is negative except for moderately enlarged tonsils and an acute catarrh. He has an IQ of 125.

History of Adjustments.—Frank is very restless at night. He wakes up every night and goes down stairs to get in bed with his parents. His afternoon naps are most irregular. Some days he sleeps four hours and some days not at all. His most restless nights follow a long nap. A further difficulty is that Frank does not mind well.

Suggested Treatment.—Mrs. French must be more firm and must worry less. The parents must insist that he sleep in his own bed. His sleep at night will probably be sounder if his afternon naps are cut short. Frank must be kept busy. He is a very bright boy and if not occupied is apt to get into mischief.

Later History.—Five months later Frank was sleeping better but was getting more difficult to manage. The suggestions given at this time were for Mrs. French to get more rest herself, to be more firm and to pay much less attention to Frank. Mr. French should be less harsh and they should try punishing the boy by isolating him. Two months later when his mother was called out of town, Frank behaved beautifully with the housekeeper. A year still later we have the report that the boys are much less problems. Their mother is feeling much better and is making more of an effort to be firm.

CASE 9. LORRAINE ROBINSON   TWO YEARS TO SEVEN YEARS
  Feeding problem, Bedwetting. Hyperactive. Distractable.
  Antagonistic toward sister. Mother possibly psychopathic.

Home Situation.—Lorraine lives with her sister Amy, who is nine years older, her mother and her step-father in a shanty in a dilapidated neighborhood. The atmosphere of the home is disharmony. Mr. Robinson is a happy-go-lucky, sociable man inclined to be alcoholic. He married Mrs. Robinson when Lorraine was a baby and seems fairly fond of them though his work as a section hand on a railroad keeps him away from home a great deal. In Mrs. Robinson's family there has been considerable nervous instability and some feeblemindedness. She herself is evidently neurotic and probably subnormal mentally, since she volunteers derogatory information and seems unconscious of the significance of the facts she has given. Her attitude toward the children changes quickly from petting to spanking and she clearly is not controlling the situation at home though periodically by virtue of her superior physical strength, she is in power   She nags Lorraine and quarrels with Amy. Amy is very emotional and shows egocentric paranoid traits. The two children quarrel almost without intermission.

Developmental History.—Lorraine cried and whined almost constantly for her first year. Her food did not agree with her and diarrhoea persisted till she was two. She gained in weight slowly, had measles and many colds. She walked at thirteen months and talked a little at eighteen months. She is restless and talks, mumbles and cries out in her sleep. Her appetite is rather poor and she has always been underweight. She tends to be left handed. Her IQ at the age of five was 127.

History of Adjustments.—In the study of this case we have a great deal of "follow-up" work and we have recorded the main facts and symptoms as they have occurred at the dates indicated.

Jan., 1920. Mrs. Robinson brought Lorraine to the clinic for advice about her poor appetite and bed-wetting. She was advised to be more firm in her control of the child, refuse desserts till vegetables were eaten, etc. Lorraine will probably gradually acquire bladder control.

April, 1920. Lorraine is outdoors more now and her appetite has improved.

Oct., 1920. Lorraine's appetite continues to improve, but she is still wetting the bed. The clinic gave advice about limiting liquids taken in the afternoon and taking the child to the toilet during the night. She should be encouraged to play with other children.

Nov., 1920. Lorraine is rather hard to manage and her mother evidently is not at all firm with her.

Feb., 1921. Lorraine is behaving better. Mrs. Robinson says she has been more firm with the child.

May, 1921. The mother has improved in her attitude and Lorraine is now easier to handle.

Sept., 1921. Lorraine's sister Amy has become very antagonistic toward the child and seems largely responsible for Lorraine's reticent, shy manner. Lorraine is now attending the kindergarten at a settlement house.

Nov., 1921. The kindergarten teacher says that Lorraine has shown great improvement.

Dec., 1921. Mrs. Robinson suspects her neighbors of bearing a grudge against her. She is very unhappy. Lorraine has frequent colds and illnesses.

June, 1922. Lorraine now is eating better, is growing rapidly and getting aggressive. She even fights occasionally at kindergarten.

July, 1922. Lorraine and Amy are not getting along at all well together. Mrs. Robinson has overheard one doctor call Lorraine "neuropathic."

Aug., 1922. Lorraine objects to eating but knows she must. She has a tendency to be left-handed. Amy is now fourteen and is a very nervous, "shut-in" type of girl. The two sisters should be separated.

Oct., 1922. Lorraine's general condition is good. She has been nervous recently as the result of the ghost stories of the child next door.

Nov., 1922. Lorraine is now in public kindergarten and is enjoying it. She is writing mirror writing.

Jan., 1923. The child is now said to be impatient, hyperactive, and distractible. She desires approval, is almost bold in her demand for attention and strongly resents disapproval. She cannot move without remonstrances or cautions from her mother. Mrs. Robinson is very irritable and evidently fears and resents the possibility of the daughters displacing her in the father's affection. Her constant nagging seems to have resulted in a fixation of Lorraine's love on the step-father. Amy shows a definite feeling of inferiority and an unusually close mother-daughter fixation. If possible Mrs. Robinson and the two girls should all be separated.

Apr., 1923. The sisters seem to be getting along somewhat better. Mrs. Robinson should limit her threats to possibilities, should be consistent, maintain her poise, not allow the children to rule her, and if possible should send Amy to some relative to live. Lorraine is getting a little bored with kindergarten.

May, 1923. Attempts to have Mrs. Robinson receive psychiatric treatment have so far failed. Amy is now described as the "apotheosis of unhealthy discontent and disgust with life."

June, 1923. There seems to be a possibility of Mrs. Robinson's developing a real psychosis. Amy was away for two weeks and since then has been out of the home most of the time. Lorraine's behavior was much improved while her sister was gone. The antagonism between the two does not lessen.

Oct., 1923. Lorraine is now in first grade and is happier.

Jan., 1924. The antagonism between the sisters has increased since a visit to the grandmother.

Feb., 1924. Lorraine was at first forced to use her right hand in first grade but when the teacher was interviewed she said the child might use her left if she preferred.

March, 1924. Lorraine is disgusted with school, it is "too easy."

April, 1924. Lorraine is now using both hands in school.

May, 1924. Amy is still more bitter and resentful. She should be employed after school hours and live away from home. Lorraine is now in second grade. Mrs. Robinson thinks the other children pick on her.

Aug., 1924. Mrs. Robinson threatened to send Amy away if she did not stop nagging Lorraine. Amy is now working in a doctor's office. The house is unusually peaceful and Lorraine is much easier to manage.

Nov., 1924. Lorraine is once more unhappy at school. She fusses, complains and argues almost constantly. The child dislikes the teacher who makes the children stay after school a great deal. She does, however, allow Lorraine to use either hand.

Jan., 1925. Lorraine now writes with her left hand only when she is "mad" at the teacher. Attempts to separate Mrs. Robinson, Amy and Lorraine have failed so far.

CASES 10 AND 37. DONALD SHERIDAN
TWO YEARS AND SEVEN MONTHS
ELIZABETH SHERIDAN
FOUR YEARS AND TWO MONTHS

Feeding problem. Finger sucking. Sensitive. Mild Temper Tantrums. Obstinacy.

Home Situation.—Mr. Sheridan is an instructor in a college and he is at the same time finishing the work for his Ph. D. degree. The result is that he is home a very small part of each day while the children are awake. Perhaps because he is with them so little, both children mind him better than they do their mother. Mrs. Sheridan is a woman of considerable artistic ability. She was an illustrator before her marriage and seems to have a longing for the time when her children will be old enough for her to take up her drawing again. She gives the impression of being up in the clouds a good part of the time, and although she looks after the physical needs of her children, she tends to forget them when they are quiet and fails to worry even when they are gone from the house an hour or more.

Developmental History of Elizabeth.—Elizabeth was a rather fussy baby for the first five or six months of her life. She said a few words at ten months and walked at seventeen months. She has had no contagious diseases, and her only operation has been an adenectomy. She is at present in excellent physical condition. On the intelligence test she received an IQ of 128. Her speech is clear and her sentence construction good.

History of Adjustments in Elizabeth.—In various ways Elizabeth has proved to be a mild problem. Desirable toilet habits were not established until after the age of two. She has always been a feeding problem, though she is somewhat better lately. The trouble seemed to be partly lack of appetite and partly dislike of vegetables and eggs. It is definitely not a case where the child desires to be fed by her mother, for she objects decidedly when any adult tries to force the food upon her. She is very fond of sweets and the greatest inducement toward the consumption of vegetables is to bribe her with the dessert and to make clear that the dessert cannot be obtained until the vegetables have been eaten. Mrs. Sheridan has tried also naming each spoonful for particular friends of the family "here goes Ralph," etc., but this method has had a very temporary effect. Elizabeth is rather timid with animals, but she is willing to approach within a reasonable distance if an adult will go along and take her by the hand. She sucked her fingers for nearly two years, but her mother cured her in about two months by putting bitter aloes on her fingers and by sitting beside her when she was put to bed and removing her fingers every time they were put in her mouth. When she is provoked, she retreats to a corner and cries or sulks. She seems to be unusually sensitive, and strangers have the greatest difficulty finding out what the child is crying about. Sometimes, it is that someone has laughed at her, and sometimes that the other children in the neighborhood have started some particular play without definitely inviting her. Reasoning and explaining will often result in an improvement in behavior, but an occasional spanking has a more lasting effect.

Developmental History of Donald.—Donald was a good baby and has always seemed a happier child than his sister. He used several words at nine months, and walked by the time he was a year old. He has had no contagious diseases, and is at present in good health. On the intelligence test, he received an IQ of 122.

History of Adjustments in Donald.—Donald has never been a feeding problem. There are a few foods he refuses but in general, he is not finicky. He wets the bed about once or twice a week. When taken up at night, he becomes wide-awake and excited. He is occasionally stubborn and exhibits a mild temper tantrum when he doesn't get his own way, but under the policy of ignoring such outbursts, they seem to be occurring less often. He is in no way a boisterous child, and seems to enjoy the quieter activities more and to tend to play alone. He has considerable perseverance and will stick to one toy for an hour or more. Perhaps because most of the neighbor children are a year or so older, Donald is in no way a leader but he is ready to stand up and if necessary fight for his rights. He is fairly popular with other children and a great favorite among the adult friends of the family. He is in general very easily controlled, and if he does object violently to any course of action, he is quick to understand if his mother has no intention of changing her mind, and promptly dries his tears and obeys cheerfully. He is very methodical about everything he does, as his mother says he is a "fan for routine" and his obstinacy is most apt to appear when the regular routine is upset in some way, be it ever so slight.

Suggested Treatment.—Elizabeth needs considerable contact with other children and should be sent to kindergarten as soon as possible.

CASE 11. MABEL MILLER   TWO YEARS AND SEVEN MONTHS TO
                                FOUR YEARS AND FIVE MONTHS

Bedwetting. Refuses to nap. Laughs at punishment. Hard to manage.
   Whines. Obstinate. Eats mud. Runs away. Slaps other children.
Hyperkinetic. Lies. Poor table manners. Impulsive. Shows off.
   Slow in dressing. Bites nails. (A problem-finding mother.)

Home Situation.—Mr. Miller is a highly skilled worker who
provides a moderately well furnished home in the outskirts of the
city. He is a quiet, rather gentle man who seldom becomes nervous or excited. He is interested in Mabel and her baby brother,
and is pleasant but firm in handling them. Mabel obeys him much
more promptly than she does her mother. Mrs. Miller is very
nervous, and becomes much disturbed over trifles. As a worker
at the clinic said, "Mrs. Miller can find a problem in any child."
The baby brother has always been slow in developing and his
mother fears he may eventually be found to be feeble-minded
like a maternal uncle.

Developmental History.—Mabel was a colicky baby and her
mother began worrying about her almost the day she was born.
She walked and talked at about a year. She has frequent colds
and within the last few months has had chicken pox. She is now
well developed and nourished. On the intelligence test she received an IQ of 115.

*History of Adjustments, Suggested Treatment and Later His-
tory.*—Mabel has had such a series of problems that it seems best
to present them chronologically as they appeared.

May, 1923. Mabel still (age two years and seven months)
wets the bed every night. She is a very active child who is constantly "on the go," refuses to nap, is obstinate, and does not
obey, although she does not have temper tantrums. She insists
upon eating mud in the street and runs away. None of the many
methods of control which Mrs. Miller has tried seem to work so
she has abandoned all except spanking. Mabel persists in looking on any kind of punishment as a huge joke. She is allowed
to play with other children seldom because she tends to pick up
the slang they use and this distresses her mother.

Mrs. Miller should be more firm, should make fewer demands and should then insist that these few be obeyed. Instead of spanking so frequently she should try punishing

Mabel by placing her on a chair or by isolating her in another room. Mabel should be given less water in the late afternoon and she should be waked once during the night to go to the toilet. She should be allowed to play with other children whether she learns slang or not. The problem of no nap might be solved by undressing Mabel when she is put down for her nap. If she continues to eat mud, Mabel must wear cardboard cuffs extending above the elbow so that although she has free use of her arms, she is unable to put her hands in her mouth.

June, 1923. Some of Mabel's difficulties have cleared up though she is still wetting the bed excessively. She is very impulsive and shows few inhibitions and now slaps her playmates so that they are afraid of her. She seems pleased when scolded since she is then getting considerable attention. She is constantly active and her power of concentration seems limited. Mrs. Miller does not nag but she is easily disturbed by Mabel's actions and lays too much weight on minor offenses.

The physician prescribed atropin as an aid in curing the bedwetting. He suggested that Mrs. Miller try to find a place in the country for Mabel this summer where her activity can find expression. Meanwhile the child should be provided with more play materials.

July 1923. Mrs. Miller is now very nervous. The atropin had a beneficial effect on the bed-wetting for a time only. Mabel now seems to be getting along well playing with children a number of years older than she is herself.

The physician suggested that the atropin be omitted now. Mrs. Miller is giving Mabel entirely too much attention. She should let everything go and ignore the child and her eccentricities as much as possible. It might help the situation if Mabel were put in the care of some one outside the family for a few weeks.

August, 1923. Mrs. Miller is now quite confident that she has overcome her management problem by ignoring Mabel's trivial mistakes. Mable is getting along better with children of her own age. The nocturnal enuresis has stopped. The mother thinks this was the indirect result of the atropin. She thinks that Mabel got the "dry feeling" and realized that it was more comfortable to have a dry bed than a wet one. She is being taken up once each night when she wakes and calls her mother, and she has developed a pride in keeping the bed dry.

January, 1924. Mabel now gives little trouble with other children. One of the neighbors has even invited her to come over to play with her own little girl. Mabel's tonsils are now enlarged. Of late there has seemed to be a tendency to tell small untruths. Punishment has merely given Mabel the notion that she must always tell the truth and that she can do anything, no matter how terrible, if she only tells the truth about it afterwards. Mabel is slow in minding.

Up to this time the clinic workers had felt that the problem centered about Mabel's behavior, rather than about her mother. A social worker visiting the home overheard Mrs. Miller relating to a caller all the cute naughty things Mabel had been doing. The child herself was present at the time and vastly enjoyed the account of her misdemeanors. From this date on, the clinic stressed ignoring Mabel's conduct and advised the mother not to make the child the topic of conversation when she was in the group. Mrs. Miller was given several books on child training to read.

With reference to the specific problem of fibbing, the mother should entirely ignore the untruths and should limit her commands to a few which must be obeyed.

February, 1924. The fibbing has completely disappeared. Mrs. Miller ignored it and is now in addition not giving the child a chance to lie by asking her questions when there might be a tendency to lie. Depriving Mabel of her dessert seems to be an effective punishment at present. Her table manners are now "atrocious."

March, 1924. Mabel's table manners have improved since her mother promised to take her down town for lunch some day after she had learned to be more careful at the table. A few days ago the child tried to get attention at the table by imitating a neighbor child in refusing to eat, but when her actions were ignored she soon abandoned that behavior. The chief problem at present is that Mable persists in showing off whenever company is present. Mrs. Miller was advised to place Mabel in a room by herself away from the company if she could not be quiet in the room with them.

August, 1924. Mrs. Miller is very nervous again. This time it seems to have been brought on by the realization that the baby is definitely retarded, perhaps even feeble-minded. She feels that it is not right by Mabel to bring her up in the family with a feeble-minded child, and she is therefore considering giving Mabel away.

September, 1924. Mabel's tonsils have been removed. Her problem now is that she whines continually but Mrs. Miller is refusing to give her anything unless she can speak pleasantly.

January, 1925. Mabel is getting along nicely and her brother seems to be improving so Mrs. Miller has abandoned the idea of placing Mabel for adoption. The chief problem now is that Mabel is slow in dressing. The family are, however, going down to breakfast without waiting for her and this treatment seems to be working well.

March, 1925. Mabel is now dressing more quickly but has substituted nail biting as a method of gaining attention.

CASE 12. RODNEY HILL   TWO YEARS AND NINE MONTHS
Slight fear.   Mild feeding problem.

Home Situation.—Rodney lives with his parents and his brothers in a good residential section of the city. Although both Mr. Hill, who is an advertising man, and his wife, are extremely nervous, they are making a "desperate" effort to be calm in the management of Rodney, and are sure that it is on this account that he is of a more equable temperament than either his thirteen or his eight year old brother. The older brother has an IQ of 140, but neither of the other boys has been tested.

Developmental History.—Rodney was an exceptionally good baby, has had no contagious diseases, and not more than two colds. He walked at fifteen months and by eighteen months was using sentences of three or four words. He is in excellent physical condition.

History of Adjustments.—Rodney has never shown any serious problems. When he was twenty months old Mrs. Hill had some trouble with him because he would get so interested in his play that he would neglect to come in to the toilet. She overcame this by giving him a tiny piece of candy (without explanation and without calling it "candy") every time he urinated when placed on the toilet chair. After a month, there was no further difficulty, the child never asked for the candy at any other time, and the giving of it was gradually abandoned.

Rodney was no feeding problem until after the age of fifteen months when he began to feed himself. The novelty of the process soon wore off and he began to leave the foods which he cared for least. At such times his mother automatically and without emotion fed him the rest of the meal and he has come to assume that he is expected to eat what is set before him. A definite problem arose recently when the family changed from canned to fresh spinach. Rodney objected to the unfamiliar flavor and although he opened his mouth when a spoonful approached, he would refrain from swallowing until his mouth was so full that he couldn't swallow. At this point the food would have to be removed from his mouth and the feeding would start again. Rodney soon hit upon a remedy himself and that was to take a taste of well-liked food immediately after a mouthful of spinach. After a month of difficulty in eating the fresh spinach, Rodney now eats it with perfect readiness and without comment. Now whenever a new food is introduced he takes a mouthful of the new food and then one of some old favorite.

There has been no history of fears of any kind until the last month when Rodney has been seen repeatedly to back away from a particular neighbor cat. Mrs. Hill reports that for several years a pair of brown thrashers have nested in the corner of their porch roof, and that one year this neighbor cat caught some of the baby birds. In an attempt to prevent a similar calamity this year the family have united in driving the cat away whenever she approached. Rodney now avoids this particular cat, without showing any withdrawal reaction to other cats.

Within the last few months Rodney has acquired a habit of screaming all remarks which he addresses to his father. Mrs. Hill explains this by saying that when Mr. Hill is at home he is often engrossed in a book and fails to hear the child when he speaks in an ordinary tone of voice.

Cases 13 and 59. MERRILL HOLDEN Two Years and Nine Months
                  JAMES HOLDEN   Five Years and No Months

Meticulous. Fears. Thumb-sucking. Fatigue. Jealousy.
            Hyperactive.   Negativistic.

Home Situation.—The paternal grandfather of these boys was
the "black sheep" of a remarkably fine family. He was lazy, shiftless, and married a chambermaid of a hotel in which he was doing janitor work. He was intoxicated frequently and upon these
occasions exhibited a violent temper. This grandfather lived with
the Holden family until James was two years old. Mr. Holden
is a very quarrelsome man who was dismissed from one position
for petty dishonesty. He obtained a divorce from his wife just
before the birth of Merrill. Mrs. Holden is an irresponsible
woman with a questionable reputation and a violent temper. At
the time of the divorce she was given the custody of the children.
When Merrill was three months old his mother gave consent for
his adoption by a Mr. and Mrs. Frost although she was unwilling
to give up James. This child she placed in a boarding home and
she has never taken any great amount of responsibility for him.
The result has been that James has lived in a constantly shifting
environment as his mother has moved him from one boarding home
to another. During the first few years of his life, the boy lived
at home and was frequently present at violent quarrels between
his parents. His physical care and training were both neglected.
When he was two, he lived for a time with a boarding mother,
then with an aunt, then with his mother again. At this time he
was left at home each night while Mrs. Holden worked. When
she returned in the morning she was too weary to get his breakfast
or to supervise him at all until afternoon. The child would fall
out of bed and play around on the floor hungry and dirty. After this he was with another boarding mother, who took good
physical care of him, but indulged his every whim and allowed
him to develop capricious eating habits. Here he was constantly
over-stimulated by movies and visits, and imbued with an almost
fanatical religious fervor. A year ago, James was shifted to another boarding home. He is now with the Frosts who adopted
Merrill and who are anxious to adopt James as well. Mr. Frost
is a travelling salesman, frequently away from home. He is very

fond of both the boys and probably indulges them when he is at home. Mrs. Frost gives considerable time to the children although she seems less sentimentally attached to them than is her husband. She admits that she is probably hypercritical of James and may expect too much of him when he has had no opportunity for training. She also acknowledges that she cannot help watching him for the undesirable traits of his parents. On the whole, Mrs. Frost seems unusually wise and patient in handling the situations that arise.

Developmental History.—Little is known of James' development save that at the age of six months he had a prolapse of the rectum which is now cured and that he has had measles. He is now in excellent general physical condition. In the intelligence test he received an IQ of 117. Merrill has had no contagious diseases and was a fussy baby. His physical examination at present is negative. His intelligence rating is probably around 100 though he was so shy that a complete examination could not be given.

History of Adjustments.—James has a good appetite now. Before coming to live with the Frosts his diet was limited to potatoes, bread, milk and sweets, but in the last few months he has been learning to eat many other things. He is inordinately careful about his personal appearance, demands clean clothes when the others are slightly disordered, and seems happiest when dressed up. In spite of this he refuses to dress himself. He seems to fear all sorts of animals but is ashamed to acknowledge it and tries to cover it up. Thumb-sucking is a well established habit, and adhesive tape has been used without avail for he merely selects another finger to suck. Enuresis still persists. A former boarding mother tried scolding, depriving him of small pleasures, and shaming him before other children all without effect. She found it impossible to wake him fully in the night and so that method was useless also. Mrs. Frost is convinced that the habit is due to laziness, and her most successful treatment has been to make James wash his own pajamas and sheets when they are wet in the morning. After a single experience of this kind, enuresis failed to appear for a week, but since then it has recommenced. The boy seems to be making an effort himself and is always proud when he succeeds in going through the night dry. James is very anxious to go to school but Mrs. Frost has said that he cannot go until he is willing and able to dress himself. This has seemed to stimulate him for at first he lazily refused to do even those things for himself of which he was capable. He fatigues easily. James' personality seems to be a confusion of all he has encountered in his constantly changing homes. He seems to adjust slowly to the new situations, and to be puzzled by the varying demands made on him. In the next to the last boarding home he cried almost incessantly, but improved markedly after a month and was generally happy and tractable. The same was true of his actions on coming to the Frosts' home. This situation was further complicated by the presence of his younger brother. In spite of being furnished with duplicates of Merrill's toys, James showed a definite jealousy, pushed himself forward when callers came who knew his brother but not himself, and resented every experience which Merrill had had but he had not. James was at first considered lazy because he refused to pick up his toys at night. Mrs. Frost met this situation by confiscating whatever toys were left around, and under this treatment James has improved so much that now he puts away not only his own toys but helps Merrill as well. James is hyperactive and self-conscious and tends toward negativism. He is apparently in an intensely emotional state from not knowing whether his mother will consent to his adoption by the Frosts or whether in the course of a few months he will be moved on to some undesirable home. He responds well to praise and at the clinic made even a better impression than Merrill did.

Merrill is an habitual thumb-sucker upon whom all methods which Mrs. Frost has tried have failed. He is shy and dependent upon his adoptive mother. He imitates everything that is said and done by his brother, and since some of James' activities are undesirable, Mrs. Frost is more or less disturbed.

Suggested treatment.—This seems to be a case of two normal children reacting on each other in a natural sort of way. There is petty jealousy and competition for attention. James is superior mentally and more attractive physically. This may serve to antagonize Mrs. Frost who naturally feels more attached to Merrill whom she has had so long. James should be sent to kindergarten at once. Mrs. Frost should undertake to break him of the thumb-sucking without fixing his attention too strongly on the habit.

Later History.—Two months later Mrs. Frost reports that James is enjoying kindergarten greatly. She has been gently removing his fingers from his mouth after he goes to sleep, and has provided both boys with clay pipes to play with in the day time without in any way suggesting a connection between them and the finger-sucking. They have been delighted and of course as long as the pipes are in their mouths, the fingers are not. Mrs. Frost hopes the pipe interest will last long enough to cure the other habit. Mrs. Holden has at last given permission for James' adoption, the papers have been filed, and the boy seems much more stable emotionally.

CASE 14. CHARLES SHORT   TWO YEARS AND TEN MONTHS

Easily excited. Unstable attention. Nailbiting. Stutters. Vindictive.
Handles Genitals. Plays poorly with other children.

Home Situation.—Charles lives with his parents and a ten year old boy cousin in a pleasant bungalow on the outskirts of the city. Mr. Short is employed as cook in a bakery. He is an even-tempered man who apparently handles Charles with considerable intelligence. Mrs. Short is much interested in her home and son and has the general family welfare so much at heart that this year she has taken charge of a cousin whose mother died. The cousin has always been more or less of a management problem, but behaves better with Mrs. Short than he did with his mother. Mrs. Short has been somewhat distressed at having Charles adopt some of the undesirable habits of his cousin, yet has felt a duty toward the other child and has put forth considerable effort on improving his behavior. The situation is a temporary one only, for the cousin's father is expecting to marry again shortly and the boy will then leave the Shorts.

Developmental History.—Charles has always been exceptionally well and has had no contagious diseases. Altho his tonsils and adenoids were removed soon after he was two, he is still frequently a mouth breather. He is large for his age and in good condition. On the intelligence test, he received an IQ of 114. His speech is rather indistinct.

History of Adjustments.—Charles presented few problems before the coming of his cousin and he usually obeys well. He still wets the bed unless he is taken up once during the night. His appetite is exceptionally good, and the chief difficulty here is that Charles eats too rapidly. His attention flits from one thing to another. If not stopped, he will investigate everything within reach. He bites his nails and occasionally handles his genitals in imitation of the cousin.

When Charles becomes angry he "takes it out" on another child or on the particular toy which has exasperated him. If he bumps his head on the table he is apt to say "I break the table" and kick it again and again. One day when riding a kiddie-kar around the house his foot got caught in the wheel and he upset. He hopped up with an angry expression and started kicking the kiddie-kar. At the first kick he began to cry and as he hurt himself more with each kick he cried harder. After he had kicked the vehicle eight times he sought his mother saying "bad kiddie-kar hurt me." He is an exceedingly active child in an awkward way, gives great leaps and jumps and strides, and often bumps into furniture. He is not in general a leader, but younger children are somewhat fascinated and try to imitate him when he knocks things down with a smash. He is easily excited and varies from a nervous talkativeness to a sad, crying state. He plays poorly with other children, but after grabbing all their toys, if his mother explains that the others need something to play with, he is just as active in forcing playthings upon them whether they want them or not.

A year ago Charles frequently ran out into the street. Mrs. Short tried various methods in her attempt to break him of this habit. Scolding and explaining did no good at all and she was too busy to stay outdoors with the boy all the time and so was unable to stop him every time he started for the street. She finally tried spanking him every time she found him in the street. This treatment had some effect and before the summer was over she could rely on his staying on the sidewalk or in the yard. Mrs. Short feels that the improvement in behavior was due partly to the punishing and partly to his increasing age. About three months ago Charles began to stutter and this has disturbed his mother.

Suggested Treatment.—Mrs. Short should ignore Charles' stuttering and handling of the genitals. In all probability there will be an improvement in the boy's general behavior when his cousin leaves the home.

CASES 15 AND 49.   SYLVIA GUTERMAN TWO YEARS AND TEN MONTHS
                         PAUL GUTERMAN   FOUR YEARS AND SIX MONTHS

Deceitful. Lies. Impulsive. Dependent on mother. Stutters.
Finger sucking. Handles genitals.

Home Situation.—Sylvia and Paul live with their parents in an outlying section of the city. Their home is moderately well furnished and comfortable. Mr. Guterman, who owns a grocery store in another part of town, spends twelve or thirteen hours a day either there or in the streetcars. He sees little of the children; hence they are practically unaffected by his calm, phlegmatic temperament. Their discipline is entirely controlled by their mother who is tense and nervous, has migraine headaches, and is much more interested in her social life than in her children. She speaks with marked precision and sharpness and is quick to feel annoyed by the children's behavior. She is excessively affectionate one moment and the next will be almost brutal in punishment. Neither child presented any problems last year while their mother was away from home for two months.

Developmental History of Paul.—As a baby Paul was undernourished and at four months he showed definite evidence of rickets. He walked at fourteen months and talked at one year. He was a very nervous child, cried a great deal, and would waken at the slightest noise or light. His nose bleeds easily, even on the merest bending downwards of the head. He had eczema and measles at thirteen months and last winter had chicken pox. Desirable toilet habits were established at two and a half but five months ago enuresis returned, both nocturnal and diurnal, for a few days. He is at present well developed and fairly well nourished though he is anaemic, has infected tonsils, and shows severe signs of earlier rickets. He has an IQ of 130 and has an unusually large vocabulary, but he does not use his hands well and is apparently nòt so strong as most children.

History of Paul's Adjustments.—Paul sucked his finger till he was sixteen months old when his mother put tape on his fingers. Now he chews the cuffs of his blouses, probably in imitation of a feeble-minded boy in the neighborhood. Paul usually eats well. With both Paul and Sylvia Mrs. Guterman has used many and curious punishments. To the common methods of scolding, spanking and putting to bed, she has added enemas, shampoos, and doses of cod liver oil. Enemas are most dreaded. In her desire to make the punishment prompt, she has frequenty spanked Paul in the presence of other children. Now he always says pleadingly, "Wait till we get in the house." In spite of such treatment he shows a marked affection for his mother. He will nap only when she lies down beside him. They sleep together at night and Sylvia sleeps with her father. (Mrs. Guterman explained this at first by saying that she started the arrangement when Paul was recovering from chicken pox and had kept it up because he slept better with her, but the real reason proves to be that she could not bear to hear her husband grit his teeth in his sleep.) The mother has made a definite effort to push both children. She taught them to read at two and punished them when they did not know their letters.

When Paul attempts to play with two neighbor boys a year or so older, his mother often interferes saying that the older children tease him. He really cannot hold his own with the boys his own age. Several times lately he has told in detail how he "licked" another boy and she has found each time that he has been "licked" himself. Mrs. Guterman feels that the boy is getting deceitful. The other day a friend gave him five cents for a lollypop. His mother refused to let him buy one, but said he could get an ice-cream cone with the money. He had the cone charged and bought the lollypop with the money. Paul is disobedient. When his mother tells him to wash his hands, for instance, he answers "I won't, dumb-bell," and strikes her if she is nearby. Twice he has gotten scissors from the table drawer and cut both Sylvia and himself. A few days ago without apparent provocation he took a dirty shovel and struck all the clean clothes drying on the line. He is restless, not persistent, and apt to blame others for his misdeeds. He likes people, speaks to everyone on the street and is known for blocks around. He does not like to stay at home.

Developmental History of Sylvia.—Sylvia has always been well. She walked at thirteen months and talked at sixteen months. She is well developed and nourished and has an IQ of 133.

History of Sylvia's Adjustments.—Sylvia has always been a light sleeper. She sucks two fingers and handles her genital organs frequently for short periods. This worries Mrs. Guterman excessively and she encourages Paul to spy upon his sister.

For the last seven months Sylvia has been stuttering. This began, as nearly as Mrs. Guterman can recall, at the time when the child was first punished. Some months later when her mother was away from home for two months the stuttering disappeared entirely, only to begin again a few days after her mother's return. Mrs. Guterman says the child was spoiled in her absence, was allowed to do anything she wished and to have anything she wanted to eat. It was therefore necessary for the mother to discipline her more severely than ever before. The stuttering is worse after punishment but it also appears when her mother is unusually demonstrative in her affection.

Sylvia has night terrors when she yells and screams, but the next day can remember nothing of them. She is ugly and defiant when punished, and often says "Darn fool, I don't like you." At these times she is aggressive, restless and sullen. She complains of fatigue, but apparently only at periods of boredom or irritation. She is more fond of her father than her mother. She is popular with the other children and affectionate with her parents, often returning home from play to be kissed and petted.

Suggested Treatment.—It is evident that both children are living under too high pressure. Mrs. Guterman is a nervous, tense, nagging woman who shifts rapidly from trying to cram reading and spelling into the children to showing them off and lavishing great affection on them, to administering severe and unwise punishments for minor offenses. Paul apparently lies and boasts in an effort to make up for a slight physical inferiority, and he also very definitely enjoys "getting a rise" out of his mother. Sylvia's activities seem to be in large part a competition for attention for she realizes that Paul is his mother's favorite. Mrs. Guterman must try to establish a quiet orderly spirit in the home. She must discontinue shampoos, enemas, cod liver oil and spankings as punishments. She must ignore Sylvia's stuttering and tendency to handle her genitals; and she must provide constructive occupations for both children.

Later History.—Three months later Paul had entered kindergarten and was enjoying it greatly. Sylvia was stuttering less since in Paul's absence she automatically became the center of attention. Seven months later still Mrs. Guterman reports that Sylvia has entirely stopped stuttering. The child is, however, getting negativistic, and her mother says she refuses to do things "just to be contrary." Sylvia's problems will probably diminish still further when she, too, goes to kindergarten.

CASE 16. VERNON FRAZER   TWO YEARS AND ELEVEN MONTHS
Mild temper tantrums. Stutters.

Home Situation.—Mr. Frazer is a chemical engineer employed by a large manufacturing company and has always been able to provide a comfortable home and some luxuries for his family. He is an extremely good natured man who never seems to become ruffled, no matter how much confusion or trouble there may be about him. The only sign of nervousness in him is a slight stutter or tendency to repeat whole words and short phrases. This seems to occur at times when his ideas come so fast he cannot express himself quickly enough. When he is thoroughly warmed up to a topic or conversation, the speech defect disappears. Mrs. Frazer is a high-strung, intensely emotional woman who is very intelligent. She recognizes her own temperament and tries to be calm and well controlled in handling her children. The six year old brother has been somewhat spoiled in the past because his parents were childless for ten years and made much of his arrival. This child has always had the most minor of ailments treated with the utmost concern whereas Vernon has received much less emotional attention.

Developmental History.—Vernon was a good baby, never colicky. He walked at fourteen months, said his first word at eight months, and by the age of fifteen months, was using about fifty words. He has had no illnesses save whooping cough at two years and a few months later an ear condition which lasted a few weeks. He is now a well developed chubby boy with excellent health. On the intelligence test he received an IQ of 120.

History of Adjustments.—Vernon sleeps well if he is not allowed to have a nap in the daytime. If he does have a nap, he does not get to sleep at night until ten or half past. He wakes up once in the night to go to the toilet. Mrs. Frazer has noticed no evidence of dreaming until the last two months. Nights when he is restless (usually when he has had no nap) he often screams out in his sleep about dogs or about other children taking things from him, and so on. He has also given evidence of pleasant dreams by laughing aloud and giggling in his sleep. For a year or more he was unwilling to go to sleep without his thumb in his mouth, but when he was sick with whooping cough the habit suddenly disappeared and has not returned. He has never sucked his thumb at any other time of day. In spite of very careful and consistent oversight on the part of Mrs. Frazer, Vernon continued to wet himself in the daytime till the age of nineteen months and at night until the age of twenty-three months. He was trained to remain dry during the night as soon as Mrs. Frazer heard of the method of thoroughly rousing the child when he was taken up at night.

Vernon has always had an excellent appetite and does not dislike any food except spinach. Since even as a small baby he vomited whenever spinach-water was introduced into his food, the vegetable may actually have disagreed with the boy. As a small child, Vernon had absolutely no fears. He would walk into the midst of a group of barking dogs, would go upstairs in the dark for forgotten toys, and so on. But since the age of two and a half he has shown some fear. He is now a bit timid about dogs, perhaps because a neighbor's dog has often jumped up in his face. He now sometimes cries out in the evening for a light, but Mrs. Frazer thinks he is bored with lying in the dark without anything to look at. Mrs. Frazer is unwilling to say that his fears are strong. She thinks it is rather that he has "developed a reasonable caution."

At times Vernon shows a tendency to stutter in the manner of his father. He did not show this trait before he could talk distinctly. Vernon has never been a behavior problem. He had a period of biting in imitation of a neighbor boy but when his mother bit him back every time he bit anyone, the habit disappeared. Vernon is very sensitive. If his mother looks hurt, he immediately feels badly. He objects to being made forcibly to do anything. If forced, he may exhibit a temper tantrum, but he makes no trouble whatever if he is approached by a roundabout method and prepared for what he is expected to do soon. Another plan which works extremely well is for his mother to take his refusal to do anything as unimportant and for her to sit down and say "Oh well, I don't care." He then promptly does as he was asked. If he is unwilling to accompany his mother upstairs at night, she goes up alone saying "Well, you come when it's your bedtime," and then Vernon follows almost before she has reached the upper story. In general it is necessary to exert extremely little ingenuity in managing the child. Mrs. Frazer feels that his good behavior is due to a combination of an extraordinarily good physique and a very exact schedule.

CASE 17. ANDREW FULLER   TWO YEARS AND ELEVEN MONTHS
Thumbsucking.   Mild temper tantrums.

Home situation.—Andrew's father is a college professor and the family live in a well furnished house in a desirable neighborhood. They have many advantages and some luxuries. Mr. Fuller is an even-tempered man with considerable scientific as well as personal interest in his children. Mrs. Fuller is an alert, intelligent woman who is said to be an unusually good mother. She is extremely devoted to the children and tends to be somewhat over solicitous. Andrew has one sister, Priscilla, who is seven years old, rather restless at home but "perfect" at school. She exhibits considerable unconscious jealousy of Andrew and shows at times definite play for attention. Withal she is very fond and proud of her brother. The father's discipline is more effective than the mother's, partly because Mr. Fuller is with the children less, and partly because Mrs. Fuller tends to make mild threats and then not carry them out. Both parents, however, try to give a dispassionate explanation of the undesirability of what the child is doing, and assure him that if he continues in his activity, he will surely be punished in a stated way. This method is usually effective, though with Priscilla at times spanking was more effective, especially when her parents administered the spanking without emotion. The Fullers feel that they have benefited from their experience with Priscilla and that they have consequently improved their methods greatly with Andrew. To bring out the differences in method and result we will, in our discussion, refer each time to the way in which the same problem was handled in the case of the older child.

Developmental History.—Andrew gave no trouble as a baby and presented no problems. He walked at sixteen months and talked at about fifteen months though he had been using a few words before this time. Andrew has never been sick except for a discharging ear when he was a year old and tonsilitis at two. He has frequently recurring colds, which are possibly due to adenoids and enlarged tonsils. Both children are large for their age and are well nourished. Both are classified as "superior" in intelligence.

History of Adjustments.—The parents were so eager to train Priscilla in good toilet habits that they fixed her attention on the processes too much and established a tendency toward negativism in her. She would be placed on the toilet and told that she "would have to stay there till she had urinated." This treatment seemed to inspire the child with a desire to see how long she could go without urinating. Andrew learned to stay dry all night before he acquired perfect control while awake. In his case the parents have never suggested that if he drinks a large amount of liquid in the late afternoon he will be more likely to wet the bed at night. Without telling him why, they have limited the liquids when possible without having the child actually thirsty. Under this treatment he began more and more frequently to go through the night dry, but they have found it necessary to go to him the moment he wakes in the morning and take him to the.toilet. Neither child had the slightest difficulty in establishing bowel control. From a very early age both have been taken to the toilet after breakfast, but the parents have modified the procedure in the case of Andrew by never referring to the reason for his sitting there. He simply takes it as a matter of course that his bowels are to move at that time and there is no discussion, and the process is completed promptly.

Mr. and Mrs. Fuller have always been extremely regular about the children's bed-time and naps. Priscilla stopped sleeping at nap time when she was about three and a half, but she still was undressed and put to bed for about an hour. There has been no trouble about keeping her in bed at this time. She lies there quiet in body but talking and singing to herself. She is given no play-things. After about an hour she calls out "time to wake up" and is allowed to get up and be dressed in fresh clothes. Andrew still naps pretty well though he does not always sleep. Both children expect to go to bed promptly at seven and neither of them ever objects in the least. The bed time has never varied as much as half an hour. Their sleep has always been so regular and so quiet that neither of the children has ever done such a thing as fall asleep at their play, or show any other of the signs of obvious fatigue. Priscilla often calls out once in the night to be taken to the toilet and Andrew does this somewhat less often. Some months ago, the parents discovered that Andrew had a favorite blanket among his covers and that he often was still holding the edge of that blanket tight in his hands when he awoke in the morning. Later a teddy-bear was substituted by the child and a rag-doll is now his bed-fellow. He asks for the doll every night and it has always been given to him.

With neither child has there been any feeding problem. They were given all kinds of vegetables and as small children never indicated dislike for any particular food. These good eating habits were doubtless encouraged by the fact that both parents eat and like everything. Andrew still eats everything he is given but of late Priscilla has been more finicky. This has increased her mother's solicitude, the solicitude has in turn increased the child's notions and there seems to be the beginning of the common "vicious circle." Mrs. Fuller realizes this and is now trying various other methods. The one that seems most successful is placing the food before Priscilla, simply assuming that it will be eaten, and then ignoring her, even to the extent of leaving the table before she has finished her meal.

In both children there have been indications of mild temper tantrums. These appeared in Priscilla only after the birth of her brother. The most effective treatment with Priscilla has been to tell her in an unemotional tone that if she continues her actions she will be isolated; and with Andrew to ignore him and to make sure that the tantrum is never successful in obtaining his end for him. If Andrew throws a toy away with disgust, the toy is taken away entirely.

With both children the parents obtain better obedience if, when it is necessary to give a command, the command is given and the parent then goes about his own business, assuming and giving the child the idea that he is sure the command will be carried out.

As a small child Priscilla was absolutely fearless. Until the age of three and a half she associated entirely with adults and the adults were very careful never to frighten the child. When the family moved and Priscilla came into contact with other children she began to play with them "scary" plays like burglar, Indians, etc., and soon afterwards she developed a fear of going to bed in the dark. Even now she frequently asks to have the bathroom light left on when she goes to bed. Priscilla has also a great fear of feathers which the parents have been unable to trace. Andrew has exhibited no fears at all, so far.

With Priscilla thumb-sucking has been a persistent problem and is still so firmly established that it occurs occasionally when she is bored with nothing to do. In their anxiety to break her of this habit, the parents have succeeded in fixing her attention on it. They used all manner of methods (unpleasant liquids on the thumb, aluminum mittens, sewing up the sleeves of her nightgowns, and so on) but each time Priscilla understood perfectly the purpose of the appliances, and they merely kept her thoughts still more upon her thumb. She would promptly wriggle out of or suck off any appliance attached and then suck her thumb with added enjoyment. When thumb-sucking appeared in Andrew, Mrs. Fuller put on aluminum mittens at night and tape on his thumb in the daytime never once explaining the real reason, but saying "Now we will dress your thumb." This method had to be kept up not longer than a week, and then for another week or so, when Andrew gave indications of wanting to suck his thumb, his mother promptly provided him with a toy to distract his attention. He has never been told to "take your finger out of your mouth." There has been no recurrence of thumbsucking in Andrew.

CASE 18.   RUSSELL HOYT   THREE YEARS AND NO MONTHS
Feeding problem.   Night terrors.   Bedwetting.   Nailbiting.
Minds no one except grandfather.   Inconsistent and unwise training.

Home Situation.—Mr. Hoyt is a business man of considerable ability and the family live in a good residential district, have a large car, and many other luxuries. The home, however, seems to be in a constant state of turmoil. Mr. Hoyt is easily irritated, and expects to tease Russell and his seven year old brother one moment, and have them obey promptly the next. He shows no intelligent interest in the children's development and looks upon them as occasionally amusing nuisances. Mrs. Hoyt is an attractive and very entertaining woman, with the knack of telling laughable incidents in a lively manner. She is very high-strung and easily upset. She has regretted that she has no daughter "it would be such fun to doll one up, and boys are always so grubby." She apparently punishes in anger and when her mood changes is just as unreasonable in her demonstration of affection.

Developmental History.—Russell was a very fussy baby, especially after he was weaned at the age of six months. He walked at thirteen months, and talked some months later. He is now definitely small for his age, though his physical examination is negative except for enlarged tonsils which are to be removed within a few days. He refused to cooperate sufficiently to obtain an intelligence rating, but the general impression he gives is of average ability. Except for a very light case of diphtheria three months after he had had the serum, he has had no major illnesses.

History of Adjustments.—With eight or ten exceptions, Russell has never slept through an entire night in his life. He usually wakes up screaming in a rage. Mrs. Hoyt says he always seems angry, and not at all fearful. He tears around, kicks and screams in an "insane" manner. At first his mother tries to soothe and calm him but when this is unavailing, she becomes angry and "beats" him. This treatment seems to waken him completely. He then is put back to bed. Some nights he is furious about one thing, and some nights about another. Recently, for instance, he was enraged because it was dark and the sun was not shining into his room. He wets the bed every night. Mrs. Hoyt has never tried taking him to the toilet during the night. She says he sleeps so little anyway that she's "not going to wake him up when he is asleep." The same reason is given for not trying to break him of thumb-sucking when he goes to bed. Mrs. Hoyt tried cuffs for a while, but he screamed so she took them off. She scolds him and he promises not to suck them any more, but "that is all the good it does." Russell has always been a feeding problem since he was weaned at the age of six months. He has never liked milk though he drinks it somewhat more readily now. He also refuses cereals. One doctor said "make him eat" and in trying to carry out this suggestion, Mrs. Hoyt became so enraged she shook the child and after that he was "ten times as bad as ever."

Russell is fearless. At the lake last summer, for example, the child liked to lie stretched out on the edge of the dock watching the fish in the water. No method that his mother hit upon was successful in stopping this. There is no use in arguing with him at all. Spanking sometimes worked as a deterrent if given quickly enough and hard enough. Isolation is without avail and merely results in a temper tantrum. If Mrs. Hoyt is unsuccessful in warding off an approaching tantrum she "licks him good." Mrs. Hoyt used to punish Russell's older brother by giving him a shampoo because "he hated that worse than anything". An aunt has had good results with washing the faces of her children when they are cross, but Mrs. Hoyt apparently fails to see the difference between a treatment which calms the child and one which is merely something he objects to. Mr. Hoyt has no discipline at all, he gives Russell anything he wants to keep him still. It is, however, interesting to find that Russell obeys his grandfather pleasantly without the slightest hesitation or argument. Mrs. Hoyt explains this by saying that he feels his grandfather's strength and knows he is not going to change his mind. Russell has no other children to play with and has never been encouraged to find any. He is so devoted to his mother that she feels that even a temporary separation, such as a visit to an aunt, would be a cruelty. Lately he has been biting his nails almost constantly.

Suggested Treatment.—Mrs. Hoyt must, if possible, train herself to be calm, firm, and consistent. She should arrange to have Russell spend less time with her. He needs more contact with other children and would doubtless benefit greatly by attendance at a nursery school.

CASE 19. VICTOR MEEKER   THREE YEARS AND ONE MONTH

Feeding problem.   Sleeping problem.   Uncooperative parents.

Home Situation.—Mr. Meeker is a skilled machine shop worker who provides a comfortable living for his family. He is big, good-natured, and easy going. Mrs. Meeker makes a good appearance and seems capable in a practical way. On further acquaintance, however, she proves to be a bundle of unreasoning superstitions and "old wives' tales." When confronted with a situation, she can absorb no new ideas or professional opinions, but falls back on some tradition that has been handed down in her family for years. Victor is the only child and the parents lavish all their energy on him. He is not allowed to play with any of the children in the neighborhood.

Developmental History.—Victor's babyhood seems to have been remarkable in no regard. He had no serious illnesses and walked and talked at about a year. He is now well developed and nourished. He has had a cough for some time and his tonsils are enlarged. He has recently been given medicine for worms. On an intelligence test he received an IQ of 129.

History of Adjustments.—Mrs. Meeker says that Victor is in general easily managed although he is "nervous." He sometimes soils himself and at these times she punishes him severely. He has a small appetite, will not eat vegetables or fruit, and won't drink milk. He is quite restless, especially at meals and at night, and he refuses to eat at all unless he sits in his father's lap. He also refuses to sleep anywhere but with his parents.

Suggested Treatment.—Victor's parents must stop pampering him at meals, he must sit in a chair of his own, and eat without coaxing. He must be allowed nothing between meals. His plate should be cleaned at each meal. Victor might have a tube through which to drink milk. He should sleep alone. Victor should be provided with playmates his own age. His tonsils should be removed.

Later History.—Mr. and Mrs. Meeker followed the suggestions of the clinic in a half-hearted way for a day or two and since no startling effects appeared at once, they are more than ever convinced that there is no use in trying them any longer. They are evidently unwilling to let Victor go hungry when he refuses to eat at meal times and they show no intention of having his tonsils removed as the clinic advised. The situation as to lack of playmates has cleared up for itself with the advent of a new family next door. Mrs. Meeker had at this time made no effort to find desirable companions for Victor.

CASE 20. ROGER STARR   THREE YEARS AND TWO MONTHS
Restless sleep. Bedwetting. Stubborn. Unmanageable.

Home Situation.—Roger's mother is in a sanitarium with a very severe case of tuberculosis. His father is a factory hand in Illinois. Roger's brothers, one six and one a baby, are also in Illinois with maternal aunts. Roger lives in a neighboring state with his paternal aunt, Mrs. Davis. Mrs. Davis has always felt resentful toward the boy. She took him only when considerable family pressure was brought to bear on her as the aunt most able financially to take one of the children. Finally, much against her will, she agreed to take Roger, since she "could not have the responsibility of a baby and she couldn't bear an older boy." She is a very lively, talkative woman who calls herself nervous. She often says in Roger's hearing "The child is so stubborn. He won't answer half the time." Her own child is a demure little girl who has never misbehaved and who is horrified at the actions of her cousin. Mr. Davis has little to do with Roger, but occasionally succeeds in getting the child to do something by ordering him to do exactly the opposite.

Developmental History.—Mrs. Davis knows nothing of the rate of Roger's development, nor what diseases he has had. He is a mouth breather and catches cold easily. At present his nutrition is only fair and his tonsils are enlarged.

History of Adjustments.—According to Mrs. Davis, Roger's appetite is good. He is a restless sleeper and hard to get to sleep. He is stubborn and hard to manage. She can control him only by threatening him with a stick. Most of the time he plays alone. He wets the bed almost every night.

Suggested Treatment.—Roger should be given tests for tuberculosis. (These proved to be negative.) Mrs. Davis must be firm and consistent. She must not make threats which she cannot carry out. When Roger is stubborn he should be put in a room by himself till he is ready to behave well. The physician advised having his tonsils removed, and placing him on a diet for enuresis, omitting meats, eggs, sweets, and giving him no liquids after four o'clock in the afternoon.

Later History.—Four months later Mrs. Davis reports that the management problem has been greatly improved. The method of punishment by isolation was ineffective at first, but the aunt persisted and it now works well. Mrs. Davis feels that Roger inherits his stubbornness since his father is so "mulish" that he cannot keep a job for any length of time. The bedwetting continues and Roger feels badly about it.

Two months later Mrs. Davis acknowledged that she had been irregular about trying the clinic's recommendations in regard to the bedwetting. She herself feels run down and not able to care for the child any longer. The clinic advised her not to take the bedwetting so seriously and assured her that it would clear up soon. Roger is still stubborn.

Two months later the bedwetting has improved but Roger now demands constant attention, makes repeated scenes, and simply fails to submit to discipline. He does not come to meals when called. It was suggested that Mrs. Davis call Roger to lunch once, then if he failed to come within a reasonable period to put the food away and not let him have any till the time for the next meal. It seems probable that Mrs. Davis is not making any consistent effort to follow the advice of the clinic.

Two months later Roger went to one of his other aunts for the summer and there he is considered no problem at all, but a normal, delightful boy.

CASE 21. FRANCES SULLIVAN   THREE YEARS AND TWO MONTHS

Sleeping Problem.   Lisps.   Unusual fears and pains apparently copied from mother.   Antagonistic toward mother.

Home Situation.—Frances' paternal grandmother is exacting, selfish, and neurotic. At one time she was confined in a hospital for the insane. Mr. Sullivan, however, has a calm, even disposition and is usually jolly and loquacious. He is a bank cashier and is able to provide for his family comfortably. Mrs. Sullivan says she has never had a serious illness though she is at present "completely worn out, nervous, and exhausted." She is evidently over-anxious about the children and several times has changed doctors when she thought the child's case was not receiving sufficient attention. The family includes besides Frances and her parents a baby brother who is an exceptionally good child and the maternal grandmother whom Frances adores but who has little care of the child and who never interferes with her discipline or training. There seems never to be any friction in the home.

Developmental History.—Frances was an exceptionally good baby. She seldom cried and gave her mother no anxiety save for the fact that she never seemed to sleep as much as the average child. She talked at nine months and walked at eleven months. She has had no serious illness, but has never been particularly robust. About two months ago she began running into the house every now and then saying that her stomach hurt her. A week or so later she complained of pains in her legs, then of fatigue and shortly after this she commenced screaming whenever she had a bowel movement. She ran a slight temperature for ten days, seemed totally without appetite and slept scarcely at all. The physician thought the trouble might be caused by an abscess and Frances was taken to a hospital for several days. No trouble could be located and while there the child slept well and did not complain of pains. The mother had other physicians called and they all agreed that it was largely a problem of an hysterical, nervous mother who fretted a good deal about every slight pain.

They found no evidence of sleeping sickness. In an intelligence test Frances received an IQ of 116. At first she seemed in an agony of fear, but calmed down somewhat after her mother left the room. Throughout the examination she was extremely excitable and distractible.

History of Adjustments.—Frances' difficulties are very definitely connected with her mother. Mrs. Sullivan lisps and so does Frances. Mrs. Sullivan also has many fears, such as worrying that the child might die or have infantile paralysis. Frances' mother keeps telling her children how worried she is about them and Frances clearly shows more fear in her mother's presence. According to Mrs. Sullivan the child is well behaved and exceptionally neat. She plays nicely with other children. Since her illness she seems to have developed a destructive tendency and whereas she used to go to bed quietly she now screams if the light is turned out and scarcely sleeps at all. The physician has prescribed sedatives but Mrs. Sullivan has refused to give them fearing she might initiate a "drug habit." Frances has always had a tendency toward bedwetting but this could be avoided by taking her up in the night. Since her visit to the hospital, no matter how regularly she is taken up she wets the bed every night. Before her illness she ate well; now she eats practically nothing. She cried so much about having her curls combed that they were cut off. After that her disposition and general attitude toward life improved, though her eating and sleeping habits were unaffected. There seems to be some probability that at the time of her illness there was a slight physical condition present, perhaps constipation or a little too much acid in the urine, which may have caused some actual pain or irritation. Starting from this as a basis, her mental state has undoubtedly been aggravated by perhaps too painstaking examinations. Another point to bear in mind is that before the birth of her baby sister Frances was the pet of the whole neighborhood and she was perfectly well until her little sister was old enough to attract admiration and affection from friends.

Suggested Treatment.—Mrs. Sullivan must learn to cease her useless worrying and unwarranted fears. She should have more recreation outside the home and stop being the constant companion of her children. She should calmly and sympathetically insist on Frances' doing some few things, should find some playmates for the child, and should visit a kindergarten to see how children are handled.

Later History.—After a month Frances is said to be getting along better and to be sleeping better. Nine months later Mrs. Sullivan took a three weeks rest cure and was greatly improved. Frances is improving slowly but gets exhausted easily and then complains of pains. She frequently seems antagonistic toward her mother.

Case 22. WINIFRED MAXWELL   Three Years and Three Months
Early feeding problem. Early fear.

Home Situation.—Mr. Maxwell is an architect who has considerable ability but is so young and inexperienced as yet that the family income is not large. He is very much of a home man and spends all his spare time with his wife and small daughter. He is even-tempered and rarely becomes excited. Mrs. Maxwell is an excellent mother, always cheerful yet firm. Winifred minds her mother better than she does her father. Mr. Maxwell is inclined at times to criticize his wife's rulings before the child and to say there is no need of Winifred doing as her mother says. These occasions, however, are rare and Mrs. Maxwell smooths them over so that there is never any heated discussion or violent disagreement.

Developmental History.—Winifred was an exceptionally good baby, never colicky, and seldom fussy. She walked at thirteen months and had a vocabulary of about ten words at the age of ten months. She had a very severe attack of whooping cough at the age of nine months and a light case of measles at three years. Her tonsils are enlarged and infected and she has considerable adenoid growth. Except for the nose and throat condition, she is in good physical condition. On the intelligence test she received an IQ of 140.

History of Adjustments.—Winifred has played a great deal alone, and even now that she lives in a bungalow in a neighborhood with many children, she tires and seems over-stimulated if she is with other children for more than an hour or so. Her sleep is usually quiet although if she has had an exciting day she may cry out once or twice in the night. Mrs. Maxwell takes her up once each night without waking her. As a baby she was much afraid of women, particularly if they wore hats. The parents feel sure this fear was initiated at the age of seven months, one day when the grandmother's maid took care of the child. They were never able to determine the cause of the fear since the maid stated that nothing unusual had happened. During this period the child showed no fear of men and was friendly with a few women whom she knew well. If a strange woman approached she began to scream. The fear gradually disappeared, although the child was over two years old before she reached the point of never showing fear at the approach of a strange woman. The only other fear she has shown was one of loud noises which disappeared by the time she was six months old. Winifred was a "terrific" feeding problem for a time. When first given vegetables she consistently spit them out and Mrs. Maxwell as consistently fed her more. The child has never seemed to be really hungry. For a while she liked bacon well enough to eat her vegetables in order to get the bacon. When Winifred was old enough to feed herself, she rebelled, and this new form of the problem persisted until the child was nearly three years old. Mrs. Maxwell acknowledges that she has not been sufficiently firm and has not persisted in the starving method long enough to break up the child's resistance. At present Winifred eats fairly well, though she absolutely refuses spinach and soup. She has had only one temper tantrum. At that time her mother refused to pay any attention to her, and the behavior never reappeared. Deprival of privileges is successful as punishment.

CASE 23. MOLLY HOLMES   THREE YEARS AND FOUR MONTHS
     Temper tantrums copied from mother. Much formal training.

Home Situation.—Molly lives with her parents and her eight year old brother in a pleasant middle class neighborhood. Mr. Holmes is a clerk in a large department store. He takes evening courses to advance himself. This keeps him away from home a good deal but when he is there he gets along well with Molly and handles her fairly skillfully. He is in general even-tempered though he and Mrs. Holmes occasionally have an argument or discussion in the presence of the children. There is no serious friction. Mrs. Holmes is very quick tempered and the children have frequently seen her become provoked over trifles. She is shallow and superficial, without insight into her own temperament or into the effect that her own shortcomings have on Molly's life. She goes into society a great deal, is inordinately proud of Molly and greatly humiliated when she shows her "ugly disposition."

Developmental History.—Molly was a good baby though she has always been rather easily excited if anything unusual occurs in the house. She walked at one year and talked plainly at fourteen months although her parents used baby talk to her. She had pneumonia at one year, measles and chicken pox at two. She was trained in toilet habits by the time she was a year old. At the present time her nutrition and general development are excellent. In the intelligence test she received an IQ of 130 and showed excellent effort, alert attention, good observation, and great persistence. She responded to suggestions quickly.

History of Adjustments.—Since babyhood Molly has exhibited fits of temper. These have been growing steadily worse. She is now having frequent minor outbursts and about two tantrums a week. They occur when she is crossed. Molly's brother avoids her tantrums by always giving in. Her mother also avoids them when friends are present. Mrs. Holmes often takes Molly out among people. The child seems to enjoy it and is ordinarily quite well behaved, partly because her mother at these times takes pains not to cross her. When they are at home Mrs. Holmes tries not to let Molly gain anything by her tantrums but gives in sometimes when the child screams so loud that the neighbors might think she was being abused. What causes a temper tantrum one day, will apparently not irritate her at all the next. The tantrums seem not to be associated with fatigue or any particular physical condition. Mrs. Holmes says she has tried throwing cold water in her face, ignoring her, shutting her in a room alone, and so on, without avail. Sometimes a good spanking will bring her to her senses. The family are constantly worried for fear Molly will exhibit a tantrum and disgrace them. Withal the child is reasonably friendly, persistent, and orderly. She can be trusted to do little tasks around the house.

Suggested Treatment.—Since much of the child's activity is evidently governed by formal training in etiquette rather than by natural and uninhibited trials at self-expression, it would be beneficial if Molly were allowed more free play. She should be kept away from her mother's parties and thrown more with children her own age or a little older. Mrs. Holmes must be careful to give her due warning before she is required to do something so she will have sufficient time to complete the thing at hand. She should be sent to a pre-school kindergarten or nursery school.

CASE 24. LEWIS KEEFE   THREE YEARS AND SIX MONTHS
Fear. Formerly handled genitals

Home Situation.—When Lewis was six months old his paternal grandparents came to live on the second floor of the Keefes' house. The two families do not have their meals together, but other than that are together practically all the time. Of this grandmother Lewis is very fond. She has lived for many years with the conviction that she is a person of "nervous" temperament and she is sure that Lewis is also. She does, however, refrain from mentioning this fact in the child's presence. She disciplines him as much as his mother does, but is perhaps a little more inclined to scold and nag than his mother is. Mrs. Keefe is a vivacious, bubbling, up-and-down person who sometimes loses her temper and shakes Lewis when she "ought to reason with him." He is very fond of her and probably likes her better than any one else. She is more demonstrative than his father and Lewis likes to hug and kiss her. Mr. Keefe is a consulting engineer, rather reserved and quiet, but fond of the children and ready to play with them when he is home. He reads to Lewis in the evening. The boy is fond of him but at the same time a bit afraid, so that he obeys his father more quickly than anyone else. Lewis has a sister a year and a half old, toward whom he has never shown jealousy. In general they get along well together though they quarrel at times when both want the same toy. In these quarrels Lewis often gives up "because she is only a little baby." There is also a maid in the home. Both she and Lewis have been told that he is supposed to obey her and he usually does so. With so many adults in the household, Lewis has come to expect companionship all the time and he does not show the initiative of a child who usually plays alone.

Developmental History.—For the first eight months of his life Lewis had eczema. He still has traces of it, especially in winter. This made him a fussy baby. He has never slept as much as "the books say he should." He has had no contagious diseases, though he has frequent colds. He had his tonsils removed at the age of three. He walked at one year and by the age of thirteen months had a vocabulary of about twenty-five words. He is at present in excellent physical condition, tall for his age and the weight to be expected for his age and height. He has an IQ of 130.

History of Adjustments.—As a small baby, Lewis sucked his thumb. After Mrs. Keefe had put aluminum mittens on him two or three weeks, the habit disappeared. He has recently begun to put three fingers in his mouth when he is read to. Lewis was always constipated as a baby and even later when he was getting a mixed and varied diet the habit persisted. Finally Mrs. Keefe decided that the trouble was due to laziness and the fear that the bowel movement would hurt him, so when he was two and a half, she began to reward bowel movements with a piece of candy. He never had candy at any other time, the system worked beautifully and he is rarely constipated now. At the age of two Lewis worried his mother with his persistent handling of the genitals. The physician from whom Mrs. Keefe sought advice recommended circumcision, and the habit disappeared with the operation, never to return. Lewis has had two periods of "word-stammering," that is, of repeating whole words several times over. One period was at the age of two and a half, and the other just recently. Both subsided when ignored.

Lewis has had a definite fear of dogs. When he was eight months old, he was in the garden with his mother and his dog when a strange dog came up and the two animals dashed at each other. Mrs. Keefe snatched Lewis out of the way, unharmed, but much frightened. The following spring when the child was about eighteen months old, a neighbor acquired a police dog with a loud bark. Lewis would wake crying if he heard him at night or during the day; and in the daytime when the dog barked, Lewis would fly to the nearest adult saying "Big dog! Big dog!" or "Dog bark, dog bark" with every evidence of fear. He was afraid to play in his sand box near where the dog was tied. When Lewis was two, Mrs. Keefe tried to talk the child out of his fear, by telling him pleasant stories about the "dog's barking to invite other dogs to his birthday party," etc. These seemed to help the situation somewhat, but the fear persisted. For a while the dog became to him a fear-symbol. When he burned his hand on the gas stove he ran to his mother crying "Dog bark, dog bark" and he was afraid to go upstairs at dusk without a light for fear "big dog will bark." At the age of three years and three months when crossing a half-lighted room, he suddenly saw his own shadow, shied like a frightened horse, and ran to his mother crying "Big dog! Big dog!" Within the last six months, the fear has disappeared so that the dog may now bark without any sign of fear in Lewis. In spite of continued careful observation of the child, Mrs. Keefe is not aware of the factors which may have led to the reduction of the fear. It may have been outgrown.

CASE 25. ALPHONSO JACKSON   THREE YEARS AND SEVEN MONTHS

Feeding problem. Temper tantrums. Sleeping problem. Disobedient. Mother resents his negro blood.

Home Situation.—Mrs. Jackson met her husband during the world war when he came as a soldier to the army camp near her home. She had known him only a few months but her father had committed suicide and she was more or less alone, so she was ready to marry him. Some time after her husband received his discharge she discovered that his dark skin was due not to severe exposure during his former life as a sailor, as he had told her, but to the fact that his mother was a negro. The knowledge has produced a pronounced emotional reaction in Mrs. Jackson. Added to this is the fact that her husband is irregular in his work on account of drunkenness, drinks and gambles almost every evening, and has been living with another woman. He supplies so little money that his wife is forced to work out several days a week in order to keep their home, shabby and poorly furnished as it is. Mr. Jackson lacks the kinky hair and facial characteristics of the ordinary negro and is seldom recognized as colored unless he has Alphonso with him. He therefore refuses to be seen with the child. Needless to say, there is no congeniality in the home. The parents ridicule each other's friends and make each other as uncomfortable as possible. The father is seldom home long enough to have much to do with managing Alphonso and his five year old brother, but he objects to the frequent slappings which they receive from his wife. He apparently encourages the boys when they hit back at their mother and he has taught them to report spankings which have occurred in his absence. Mrs. Jackson admits that she is quick tempered and has no system in discipline.

Developmental History.—Alphonso was a fussy baby, fed when he was hungry or when his mother had time, and cared for by all the children in the neighborhood. He walked and talked at about a year. He is now fairly well developed and nourished. His tonsils were removed at 17 months. Since then he has had measles and chicken pox.

History of Adjustments.—Alphonso seems always to have been rather hard to manage but his behavior has been aggravated since his mother learned of the negro blood in the family. She decided at once that Alphonso was darker than any white child. She doesn't care much for him now. He has temper tantrums, has to be coaxed to eat, is wakeful at night and is afraid of his father who, in turn, is ashamed of him.

Suggested Treatment.—Mrs. Jackson was advised to break up the home and support the children herself without reference to the father. She was also advised to be more firm and more consistent.

Later History.—Three months later Mrs. Jackson is still living with her husband and the home conditions are getting worse. She keeps starting divorce proceedings and then taking Mr. Jackson back for "what can she do if he cries and says he's sorry?" The outlook is not promising although she claims that the children are behaving better (perhaps because it is summer and they are outdoors most of the time.)

CASE 26. PERSIS HARMON   THREE YEARS AND SEVEN YEARS
Lisps.   Finger-sucking.   Fatigue.   Dependent ·on father.

Home Situation.—Persis lives happily with her parents, her paternal grandmother, and her year old sister in a bungalow in a desirable section of the city. The grandmother is careful not to interfere with the discipline and is not a disturbing element in the home unless the fact that she lisps has an influence on Persis' speech. Mr. Harmon is nearly seven feet tall and he is very sensitive about this extreme height. He is even tempered and is more effective in disciplining Persis than is Mrs. Harmon who is easily upset and disturbed. Both parents try to be firm and they have achieved good results in the children's general behavior.

Developmental History.—During her first two years Persis presented no problems. She talked at a year and walked at fourteen months. At the age of two she had a prolapse of the rectum which has made it necessary since that time for her to recline in order to discharge feces. The pediatrician consulted has recommended an operation but Mrs. Harmon has refused in the belief that the condition will correct itself. Persis is at present well developed and nourished but her tonsils are large and infected. Her lower jaw protrudes slightly and this makes the pronunciation of "s" difficult. In an intelligence test she received an IQ of 126.

History of Adjustments.—Persis is rather finicky about food. She refuses milk and does not care for vegetables though her mother insists that they be eaten. She sometimes complains of fatigue late in the morning. For practically her entire life Persis has sucked two fingers of one hand. Several devices have been tried to break this habit but without avail. She has also always lisped. Mrs. Harmon does not think this is copied from the grandmother. Persis gets along well with other children and likes to pretend to be the baby when they play house. She is a very active child and into everything, pulling out the contents of drawers and cupboards.

Since the birth of the baby sister Mr. Harmon has cared for
Persis during the night. This means that she has wakened him
three or four times each night fo take her to the toilet. It is
interesting to note that recently when the father was away from
home for a few weeks, she made no request whatever to get up
during the night. Upon Mr. Harmon's return, however, the
habit reappeared.

Suggested Treatment.—Persis must be trained to be more independent. Her parents should at present ignore her speech and
later on her teeth should be straightened. She should have her
tonsils and adenoids removed and should have an operation for
anal prolapse.

CASE 27. LOIS SINCLAIR   THREE YEARS AND EIGHT MONTHS
   Fearful. Unhappy. Repressed. Feeling of inferiority. Jealousy.

Home Situation.—Both of Lois' paternal grandparents are
known as excitable, high-strung and nervous. Mr. Sinclair, himself, is calm and seldom ruffled. He is a busy and prosperous
physician and sees the children little except on Sundays. When
he is with them, the atmosphere is somewhat tense for he is very
strict and firm and has only to speak to get perfect obedience.
He seems, however, to be very fair and consistent for he never
shows any temper and never changes his mind. He has
occasionally spanked them, but not often. Lois seems to be constantly on the alert for fear she will miss some command of her
father's and thus incur his displeasure. Mrs. Sinclair goes into
society a great deal. She is not tense or particularly emotional
and takes the children fairly objectively although she appears to be
very fond of them. She is less strict than their father and she
has less control. Both parents have more or less laughed at Lois'
peculiar traits in an effort to cure her of them. They acknowledge that it has been impossible not to give the baby brother
more attention since he is a much more attractive personality
than his sister. He is said to be her exact opposite with lots of
activity, curiosity and initiative. He always sticks up for himself, is not sensitive, is vivacious, cheerful, happy, and friendly
with strangers. The physical environment of both children has
always been good and they have many advantages.

Developmental History.—Lois was a nervous, fussy baby who was somewhat mal-nourished and was diagnosed as rickety at the age of one and a half years. She is still slightly knock-kneed. She walked at fifteen months but was slow in talking. She started to talk before she was two, but when her parents laughed at her funny pronunciation, she stopped and refused to say another word until six or seven months later when she could pronounce fairly well and use complete sentences. In this period of silence she developed a very complete and adequate sign language. Except for a light case of measles last year, Lois has had no contagious diseases. Her tonsils and adenoids were removed a few months ago. Since that time she has been somewhat more energetic. She is rather large for her age and appears well developed and nourished. On the intelligence test she received an IQ of 115. She has rather poor motor control and does not handle a pencil well.

History of Adjustments.—Lois has a good appetite but is afraid to try new foods. There has been no nail-biting, thumb-sucking or stuttering. Lois' whole attitude from babyhood up has been one of extreme caution and a cringing fear of every new experience and physical force. She is afraid of thunderstorms in spite of the fact that the rest of the family enjoy them. She has never liked jouncing or roughness. If the cat happens to scratch her arm, Lois never forgets and goes around holding the arm very carefully, and calling everyone's attention to the scratch for several days. Mr. and Mrs. Sinclair have laughed at Lois in an attempt to persuade her to ignore minor hurts, but without avail. The child shows no resentment at their ridicule, but neither does she change her own reaction. Mr. Sinclair attempted to teach Lois her letters, but she became so upset emotionally he stopped. She does not object to being alone and seems quite self-sufficient. She is never original and never thinks up new things to do. She gives the impression of being much too well repressed for a normal child of her age, and she has such a reflective, solemn manner that an uncle has nicknamed her "Sphinx." Lois never seems happy and often seems discouraged. She gives up easily and perhaps on this account appears interested in nothing. At the birth of the baby brother she showed considerable jealousy, though she is now proud of him and likes to help him. She is, however, frequently mean about his playthings and the only sign of self-assertiveness which Lois shows at all is in wanting every toy which he happens to be playing with. She is always slightly amused when he is punished. At times she seems to be passively obstinate and then neither spanking, sending to bed or deprivation of privileges will induce her to do what is wanted. She will take very severe punishment stubbornly without shedding a tear.

Suggested Treatment.—Lois' trouble seems to be a combination of too high and too strict standards of behavior on the part of the parents and a jealousy of the brother. Mr. and Mrs. Sinclair must realize that they are driving the child into herself by their ridicule and their extravagant demonstrations of affection toward the baby brother. If possible Lois should be sent to a nursery school or a pre-kindergarten school where she will mingle with other children and where her feeling of inferiority will not be increased.

CASE 28. CARRIE HALE   THREE YEARS AND EIGHT MONTHS
Feeding problem. Nervous. Cries easily. No playmates.
Interfering grandmother.

Home Situation.—Carrie's family have been living with the paternal grandparents and an aunt for the past year and the atmosphere of that home is tense and somewhat strained. The aunt is extremely nervous and the grandmother is a hyperkinetic, nervous, finicky woman who enlarges on everyone's ailments. The father himself, who is an expert telegrapher, is nervous and a finicky eater. He is, however, good natured and fond of Carrie and her baby brother. Mrs. Hale is a pleasant, calm woman who seems fairly firm. The children mind both parents well.

Developmental History.—Carrie was a restless baby. She walked at fourteen months and talked at seventeen months. She has never had a good appetite. The physical examination was negative except that nutrition was rated as only "fair."

History of Adjustments.—Mrs. Hale says Carrie has always been a nervous child who cried easily. She sleeps soundly and is not difficult to manage. The main problem is her poor appetite and the fact that she has to be fed if she is to eat a reasonable amount. Mrs. Hale has tried to starve Carrie into feeding herself, but the grandmother continually interferes with fussing, urging and bribing. Carrie has no playmates her own age.

Suggested Treatment.—The Hale family should move into a home of their own in order to separate Carrie and her high-strung grandmother. This home should be in a neighborhood where there are small children.

Later History.—As soon as the two families separated, Carrie's appetite improved. She eats better when the parents refrain from mentioning it. There are several small playmates living close by and Carrie's associations with them are most happy. She is perhaps now more fussy about details and worries over everything. This reaction may be imitated from the grandmother whom she still sees frequently.

Case 29. KATHERINE SWITZER Three Years and Eight Months
Fears.

Home Situation.—Katherine has always been surrounded by many comforts and advantages. Her father is a successful lawyer who is much interested in the development of Katherine and her year old sister. Mrs. Switzer was a college teacher before her marriage. There has been no apparent jealousy of the baby sister and the parents have always endeavored to show no favoritism.

Developmental History.—Apart from a slight tendency to sleep less than the usual amount, there is nothing of note in Katherine's early development. She has had no major illnesses and is now a rather tall, well developed sturdy child. She at present sleeps well and eats well and is not a behavior problem. Her IQ is 140.

History of Adjustments.—For about a year after Katherine began to feed herself she was a mild feeding problem, but this has cleared up since Mrs. Switzer has adopted the plan of letting her go without a meal if she refused to eat her vegetables or refused to feed herself. There have been no other behavior problems except for fears which seem to be rather easily aroused. For example, Katherine is afraid of elevators. Mr. Switzer tried to overcome this by holding her in his arms and talking to her about pleasant things during a trip up in an elevator but the child shook so and begged to be allowed to walk down instead of entering the elevator once more, that her parents now allow her to walk. The most marked fear has been of doctors. In a desire to forestall as many diseases as possible, Katherine's parents have had her innoculated several times. At the age of nine months she was vaccinated for small pox without any emotional disturbance on her part. At the age of one year eleven months she was given three doses of diphtheria toxin-anti-toxin. To the second and third innoculations she objected violently and when six months later she was given the Schick test she had not forgotten and screamed when she entered the doctor's office. A few months later when she was nearly three she was taken for her semi-annual physical examination and in spite of constant reassurance from parents and physician she cried most of the time. At the age of four years three months it seemed best to have Katherine innoculated for scarlet fever. She was taken to a different physician in a different building, but became suspicious and when she saw the needle, threw herself around so that it took four people to hold her. As soon as it was over she was her usual smiling self and laughed and chatted with the nurse. At about this time she entered a Nursery School where many physical examinations and measurements are made. In the preliminary examination, Katherine's reactions were so violent that special arrangements were made for her thorough examination. The physician was very deliberate, let Katherine entirely alone for the first ten minutes she was in the room, encouraged her to examine all instruments before they were applied, etc. In this way the examination was completed with only a few periods of sobbing. A few weeks later when prints were taken of the children's feet Katherine was fairly composed but said it tickled, and twisted about so that her prints were not clear. The next day when the nurse came to get Katherine for a new set of prints, the child flatly refused to accompany her. Coaxing was of no avail. The apparatus was brought into the room and discussed. Still Katherine hung back. Then two of the other children said, "We're not afraid. We'll go with you, nurse" and followed her out of the room. After a few moments of indecision, Katherine held up her head and announced, "I'm not afraid, either, I'll go too" and went through the print-taking without fussing. About a week later, when the nurse came for Katherine's second measurement, much to every one's surprise she followed to the examining room readily and without protest and went through the ordeal with scarcely a whimper. That the fear was not wholly dissipated, however, was shown during the night following when she cried out in her sleep "the nurse is coming! the nurse is coming! I don't want to go with the nurse!" The next time Katherine was at school she went to the examining room to have her measurements completed and was perfectly calm. With some apparent satisfaction she noticed that the other child in the room was crying and she remarked "Jennie's crying, isn't she? I don't cry." In this case, apparently, the social pressure from the other children was far more effective than adult reasonings and reassurances.

CASE 30. SYBIL SMITH   THREE YEARS AND EIGHT MONTHS

Negativistic. Early feeding problem. Over-dependent on mother.

Home Situation.—Mr. Smith is a factory foreman and the family live in a rather old house in a middle-class neighborhood. He is a thin, reserved, rather austere man who is strict and severe in theory but frequently makes exceptions in his treatment of the children. Mrs. Smith is even tempered and not easily ruffled. She believes in letting well enough alone. Sybil has a sister of seven and a brother of two whose IQ is 102.

Developmental History.—Sybil was a good baby with no outstanding difficulties until she was ten months old. At this time her first tooth appeared and for the next few months she was the cause of great worry and anxiety. Scarcely any food could be kept down, several teeth had to be lanced and there were some complications of earache and sore throat. The physicians seen at this time attributed the trouble solely to teething. From the age of ten months on Sybil has been almost wholly lacking in appetite until a few weeks ago. She had measles at a year and a half and chicken pox at three. At the age of ten months she had a vocabulary of ten words and she walked at the age of fifteen months.

At the present time Sybil is small for her age and is, in fact, little larger than her two year old brother. Sybil has an IQ of 114.

History of Adjustments.—Sybil is a child with a very distinct personality. She is very persistent and "set" in her ways. Her mother is often amused at the child's resemblance to her maternal grandmother who has always insisted that things be done in exactly this or that way. Sybil is just the same, very stubborn about seeing only one way and that incomparably better than any suggested by others. Mrs. Smith is firm when it is a question of Sybil's obeying. She spanks her occasionally. The child never seems to resent the spanking and is very desirous of "loving" her mother afterward. Spanking, however, has been unavailing with the other children.

The feeding problem has been a case of lack of appetite rather than dislike of any foods. While ill with teething, she vomited her meals frequently and Mrs. Smith feels that this was responsible for much trouble later on, for since then she has often vomited foods which she disliked. Both of the other children have remarkably good appetites and since Sybil has been outdoors so much of the time during the last month she has begun to "eat like a farm hand."

Sybil is very devoted to her mother and hates to have her away from home though neither her brother or sister object in the least. In fact, Sybil is still the "baby of the family." For example when out riding, Sybil's place is on her mother's lap. Her younger brother is a very independent sturdy child to whom Sybil is devoted. He seems in no way to resent Sybil's usurpation of his place and she has never made him suffer by her demands upon their mother. She plays with him most of the time and they get along well. For the most part her "mothering" of him has no element of discipline. Most of the children in the immediate neighborhood are older and they tend to treat Sybil like a baby. The parents recognize Sybil's over-dependence upon her mother, but they do little to modify it.

Mrs. Smith is sure that Sybil's difficulties all date from her early illness but although she acknowledges that ever since that time the child has been babied and worried over to an undue extent, she does not consider her "spoiled."

In the clinic Sybil was extremely shy and negativistic and for some time clung to her mother and refused to look at any material though she finally answered some questions. Some weeks later she utterly refused to cooperate but after an interval of three months she returned and, after a period of intermittent negativism, suddenly became highly demonstrative, embracing the members of the clinic and showing reluctance in going home.

Case 31. MARGARET MARY POHL Three Years and Nine Months
Restless sleep. Irritable with other children.

Home Situation.—Mr. Pohl is an advertising man completely absorbed in his work and his home. He is quiet and even-tempered and never becomes excited about any situation. Mrs. Pohl is well-poised and realizes that Margaret Mary and the baby brother should be handled consistently and quietly. It is a very happy home and the children are given many opportunities for play and self-expression.

Developmental History.—During her first year Margaret Mary was well and happy. She walked at one year and talked at eighteen months. Before she was two she had scarlet fever, but this seemed to leave no bad effects. Some months later she had a light case of chicken pox. A year ago she had a bad cold accompanied by a discharging ear, and ever since the ear has discharged whenever she contracted a cold. Her physical examination at the present time is negative except for the ear condition. In the intelligence test she received an IQ of 111, and showed unusually good cooperation.

History of Adjustments.—For the past year or more Margaret Mary has not been sleeping well, and has been crying out at intervals during the night. A few weeks ago Mrs. Pohl realized that at these times the child was talking about various characters in the stories she had been read that day, so the mother tried

the plan of omitting story-telling for the next few days. The
dreams apparently disappeared only to reappear when story-telling was resumed. Mrs. Pohl has, therefore, decided to abandon
the stories entirely till her daughter is considerably older. Margaret Mary has a small appetite but is not finicky about her food.
She likes milk and all vegetables. She has always been very
fond of adults and until the last few months she got along well
with other children. At that time the home situation changed
considerably. An aunt died suddenly leaving three small children,
aged four, three and two, and Mrs. Pohl took these children into
her home till their father could make some permanent arrangement for them. Since he has now been called to South America
for six months or more, Mrs. Pohl thinks that the children may
remain with her for a year. All three of the cousins are exceptionally brilliant children with IQ's about 140. Mrs. Pohl has
failed to recognize the intellectual difference between Margaret
Mary and the others and has unintentionally compared the children to the detriment of her own daughter. She has then tried
to urge Margaret Mary on to take her place as a leader in the
group. The child has reacted to this overstimulation by becoming very changeable, easily discouraged, restless and easily
fatigued. There is the added factor that Margaret Mary is compelled to share her playthings to a greater extent than ever before. She frequently resents having her toys touched and is
irritable when the others interfere with her play. She has also
acquired a whine which seems affected by neither ignoring nor
jollying.

Suggested Treatment.—Margaret Mary must not be over-
trained since slight things seem to produce a marked effect on
her. The atmosphere of the home must be as calm as possible.
If it is possible for Mrs. Pohl to provide the cousins with other
toys, the atmosphere will probably become less strained. Margaret Mary should share some of her toys, but it is hardly fair
to expect her to allow her toys to be used all the time.

Later History.—Mr. and Mrs. Pohl are now avoiding all comparisons between the children and no longer urge Margaret Mary
on. This treatment seems to be having good results.

Case 32. IVAN SUMNER   Three Years and Nine Months
Fears. Quarrels with other children. Capricious appetite.

Home Situation.—Ivan lives with his parents in a pleasant suburban district. Mr. Sumner is a prominent officer in a large department store and is much interested in his work. His disposition is in general calm and soothing altho he gets nervous if he is sick, and he occasionally gets excited over the behavior of his son. Mrs. Sumner is restless and nervous and throws herself into work and play with equal energy. Soon after Ivan's birth, she spent two years in a tuberculosis sanitorium. Now that she has been discharged, she has fairly good health altho she fatigues easily. When she is tired, she is easily irritated at Ivan and he then gets still more excitable and uncontrollable. While Mrs. Sumner was at the sanitorium, Ivan and his father lived with the paternal grandparents. His grandmother took good physical care of the child but spoiled him and made absolutely no attempt to train him in correct habits. He has never been taught to obey or to be regular about anything. He has always been surrounded by many adults who were ready to countermand each other's orders. The result of inadequate and inconsistent discipline and utter lack of training is that Ivan appears feeble-minded. Now that his mother is home again, she is trying to be firm and consistent with him, but she is over anxious and is almost helpless as the result of frequent interference of other adults.

Developmental History.—Ivan was a good baby but was exceedingly active. He walked and talked at about 15 months. He has had no serious diseases except influenza last year. After that, he seemed listless for a time. He fatigues easily and occasionally gets red spots under his eyes, which are then puffy and swollen. He talks in his sleep. His physical examination is negative save for signs of early rickets. In the intelligence test, Ivan's rating of 107 was thought to be rather low as he was flighty and paid less attention to directions than the average child of his age. He showed unusual manual dexterity. Thruout the examination, he seemed generally apprehensive and mildly suspicious.

History of Adjustments.—Ivan has been gradually accumulating a number of behavior difficulties. His appetite is capricious and he balks at vegetables. This worries his parents. He has an unusual fear of doctors though he has never been hurt by one. He is also afraid when he is shut up in the bathroom for punishment. This fear is intensified if he turns on the water and gets to thinking that it might flood the floor. He puts everything he gets into his mouth—dirty paper, cardboard, etc., and chews it without discrimination. He takes candy away from other children and then when they cry, he feels badly about it. Yet next time, he does the same thing again. Recently he has all but precipitated a neighborhood "row" by hiding another child's wagon and denying all knowledge of it. He refuses to stay in his own yard, yet when he joins the other children, he immediately begins to squabble with them. If he goes calling with his mother, he handles and investigates everything in sight.

Suggested Treatment.—Mrs. Sumner should watch for signs of fatigue in Ivan and if they appear, see that he gets sufficient rest. Her discipline must be consistent and firm. She should send him from the table if he does not eat. Ivan should play with older children.

Later History.—The results after ten months are negative. Mrs. Sumner is not following directions, feels that the child should not miss a meal, etc.

CASE 33. CALVIN STICKA   THREE YEARS AND ELEVEN MONTHS
Feeding problem. Fatigue.

Home Situation.—Mr. Sticka is a waiter in a hotel dining-room. He is an Armenian who, in spite of being fairly intelligent, still evidently retains many of his "old country" notions of children and the family. Mrs. Sticka is an American girl who has an exceptionally sweet disposition and apparently has a great respect for her husband. She is very cooperative and much interested in the development of her son. She says she is not very well and often gets nervous.

Developmental History.—Calvin was a fairly good baby. He had small-pox when he was a year old and one convulsion when he was two and a half. He has a very poor appetite and has not gained in weight during the last year. At present he is somewhat underweight and his tonsils are enlarged and infected. He catches colds easily, but gets over them easily too.

History of Adjustments.—Calvin has always had rather a poor appetite and the feeding question is complicated by the fact that he has decided likes and dislikes in food. Most of all he dislikes vegetables. In fact, he refuses to eat them at all unless his mother feeds him. Once in a long time, the promise of a reward will persuade him to feed himself. He also seems to tire easily. Since the family live in a three room apartment on the third floor, Calvin gets practically no opportunity to play outdoors.

Suggested Treatment.—If Calvin refuses to eat a meal, he should be given nothing till time for the next meal. He should be given straws through which to drink his milk. If starving does not work, Calvin might be given a scrap-book and stars to paste in when he feeds himself his own vegetables.

Later History.—Two months later Mrs. Sticka reports that the starving method failed because Calvin would go to play with other children and would be fed cookies and candy at their houses. The Stickas have now moved to a small bungalow on the outskirts of the city and since Calvin gets outdoors so much more and is playing more with other children, his appetite has improved somewhat. He still demands considerable attention and his mother is still feeding him part of the time. After the lapse of another eleven months, Mrs. Sticka reports that she has hit upon a new aid in Calvin's feeding problem. She now lets him go to the grocery store himself for the day's vegetables. He then seems to take a personal interest in them, watches their preparation and cooking and eats a fair amount without complaint. Nine months later Calvin is in kindergarten. He is eating his vegetables fairly well but rebelled at cereals until Mrs. Sticka began letting him choose which cereal he will have cooked each day. Under that plan the cereals are eaten quickly and without comment. He has now adopted the habit of biting his nails. His mother was advised to keep him so busy he would forget the nails. Three months later Calvin is eating very well and the nail-biting has disappeared since the weather has become warm enough for him to play outdoors all day. Two months later Mrs. Sticka says the child is now so fond of cereals that he feels badly if for some reason his mother fails to cook some. He is no longer a problem and his physical condition is excellent.

Case 34. OSCAR WOOD   Four Years and No Months
    Stubborn. Disobedient. Fears. Night terrors. Hyperkinetic.
                    Imaginative. Nervous father.

Home Situation.—Oscar comes from a middle-class, rather high-strung family. Both his grandmothers and his father have had "nervous breakdowns." Mr. Wood is still nervous though he is good natured. Mrs. Wood is irritable and she loses patience easily. Both Oscar and his two year old brother mind their father better than their mother. The family life seems wholesome, normal and happy. Complications arise occasionally, though, because of the paternal grandmother who lives directly across the street.

Developmental History.—Oscar was a quiet, contented baby. He talked at ten months and walked at thirteen months. He had measles and chicken pox at three years and whooping cough at four. He is well developed and fairly well nourished. He has an IQ of 132.

History of Adjustments.—Oscar has a poor appetite. Mrs. Wood says he has always been contrary and stubborn. He often refuses to do as his mother asks unless she threatens him with a switch. When Oscar is over-tired or when he has missed his nap he is likely to have night terrors. He developes fears of all sorts rapidly. At present he is afraid to be upstairs alone, even in the daytime although it formerly did not disturb him in the least. Recently he was taken to a dental clinic and became so alarmed that he screamed and resisted to such an extent that the dentist failed to get even the mirror into his mouth. Two days later when Oscar accompanied two other boys on their visit to the same dentist, he watched them first and then gladly consented to having his own teeth examined. He is very imaginative, over-active and usually plays with boys older than himself.

Suggested Treatment.—Mrs. Wood must be more firm, must enforce rest periods, give fewer commands, and ignore his contrariness. Oscar is to have a scrap book in which he enters stars for meals he has eaten well.

Later History.—Three months later Oscar is eating better and his general behavior is better by spells. After another four months Mrs. Wood says the boy is much easier to manage. She can now reason with him and she finds that punishing by isolating in another room is working well.

CASE 35. GEORGE POLLOCK   FOUR YEARS AND ONE MONTH
Feeding problem. Nail biting.

Home Situation.—George's father is a research worker in a large industrial plant and provides many luxuries for his family. Mr. Pollock is an easy-going, very indulgent man who has never been known to insist on the children carrying out any one of his commands. He recognizes this trait in himself and endeavors to avoid a position where they would openly defy or disobey him. Mrs. Pollock is easy-going and even-tempered; she is also inconsistent in discipline and uses poor judgment in handling her children. A sister of fourteen is in no way a behavior problem, but the brother of sixteen tends to be nervous and resents discipline. He plays with George a great deal and can persuade him to do almost anything. Mrs. Pollock spoiled this boy as well as George and he hates her now.

Developmental History.—George was a good baby, had none of the common children's diseases, and until he came to the table to eat with the family, presented no problem. He walked at ten months and talked at one year. At the present time, he is well developed and nourished. He has an IQ of 147 and during the examination showed initiative and self-control. He lisped and occasionally stuttered, tending to slur his words in a baby fashion.

History of Adjustments.—When George first began to eat at the table with the family, his father was much entertained and started the habit of playing with him. This has continued till now the boy apparently considers the dining table as a place for entertainment. He has never been known to eat a complete meal without help or to sit quietly through the meal. Mr. Pollock sees no reason why the child shouldn't play at meals when he wants to. If his mother attempts to force food upon him, George will frequently vomit all he has eaten. He is willing to omit breakfast for many successive days and if allowed milk, doesn't care to eat much at the other meals. The only time he seems hungry is when he wakes up at 11 or 12 o'clock at night and asks for food. This his mother has never refused and she then feeds him herself. Later in the night, he usually wakens again and is taken to the toilet. After this, he gets into bed with his mother, remaining there the rest of the night. George has recently taken up the habit of nail biting. He is in general a quiet child preferring dolls and books to more lively amusements. He is very affectionate, loves attention, and loves to be petted. When in a strange place, he asks an almost unbroken stream of questions.

The kindergarten teacher says George is the worst problem in the class. When he does not like her criticism, he says he is going to China the next day. Then he stays out of school, and when he returns, he insists that he has been to China and describes the trip.

Suggested Treatment.—Mr. and Mrs. Pollock must agree on the child's treatment. Perhaps ignoring his poor eating habits would work, or perhaps giving him a chart with stars for meals well eaten would be beneficial. He should no longer be treated as a baby by any member of the family. George needs the association and competition of other children.

Later History.—It has been impossible to change Mrs. Pollock's attitude.

CASE 36. HELEN ARMSTRONG   FOUR YEARS AND ONE MONTH
        Apparently poor motor control. Clumsy. Poor vision.

Home Situation.—Helen lives with her parents, an older sister and a younger brother in a fine home in the best residential district of the city. Her father is a prominent executive in a large manufacturing company and is very much interested in vocational psychology. Mrs. Armstrong is the daughter of an importer and was brought up abroad. Both parents have considerable social distinction, are unusually intelligent, are much interested in their children, and have built up a satisfactory and pleasant home life. Instead of turning over the control of her children to servants, the mother has consistently looked upon their care and management as her own work.

Developmental History.—Helen has had the best type of physical care and has always been well with the exception of a mild attack of whooping cough. She walked before she was a year old and talked shortly after. She is in good physical condition and somewhat large for her age. On the intelligence test she received an IQ of 130, her speech was distinct and her vocabulary exceptionally large.

History of Adjustments.—The Armstrong children have presented few behavior problems or difficulties. Helen early established control of eliminative processes and has had a good appetite. She has been rather easily managed due to her pleasant disposition and freedom from emotional outbursts. She has shown great capacity for self-entertainment, through her imagination. She has had a number of imaginary playmates and makes up long stories which she realizes are not true. Shortly after Helen began to walk, her parents became quite concerned about her awkwardness. She constantly stumbled or fell down or ran into objects about the house. When it seemed certain that she would miss a chair, she would bump into it. Because of Helen's inaccuracy, Mrs. Armstrong was very much afraid to let her go up and down stairs although she had early taught the sister to go up and down. When other small children came to play, Helen was clumsy and inept. A great deal of the time the child had bumps and bruises on her head and body where she had run into this thing and that. At first her parents had thought it was due to her inexperience; later, as the child developed, they realized that she was not developing motor skill as did other children. They were also somewhat concerned over Helen's unawareness of the situation. Advice was sought without particular success. The child was not a problem physically nor was she a problem mentally except for this consistent awkwardness.

When Helen was four years old, a new acquaintance noticed the child's behavior and ventured the suggestion that it might be due to some visual deficiency. Mr. Armstrong for years had worn glasses for marked myopia and astigmatism, one eye in particular being almost useless. In the father's family there was a consistent record of visual deficiency.

On taking Helen to the ophthalmologist, it was discovered that she was very near-sighted and had other refractive difficulties. Glasses were provided and within a relatively short period of time much of the clumsiness and ineptitude disappeared.

CASE 37. ELIZABETH SHERIDAN   FOUR YEARS AND TWO MONTHS
    (see case 10)
CASE 38. SANFORD LEE   FOUR YEARS AND TWO MONTHS
        Shy. Fears. Feeding problem.

Home Situation.—Mr. Lee is proprietor of an orchard some miles out of town. He is a successful man, with many friends. He is devoted to his family and the nature of his business makes it possible for him to see a good deal of his children. The family dinner is at noon and Mr. Lee always plays with Sanford afterward. On Sundays the family either goes out to dinner or entertains friends whose children are the same age as the Lee children. Mrs. Lee is an exceptionally fine woman, well poised, equable in temperament, calm, and farseeing. She constantly applies what she learns. Sanford's nine year old sister Bertha shows the effect of the pleasant, harmonious atmosphere in which she has been brought up.

Developmental History.—Sanford was a good baby in spite of several severe illnesses. At seven months he had a serious intestinal trouble requiring operation and while still convalescent he caught whooping cough. Then at the age of fourteen months he had measles. He walked at fifteen months and talked at eighteen months. At the present time he is in good physical condition and is large for his age. He has an IQ of 145.

History of Adjustments.—There are no other children of Sanford's age in the neighborhood, though he enjoys playing with his sister's school friends and gets along well with any children who come to visit at his home. For the most part, however, he plays alone or with his sister whom he adores. They have very few squabbles and enjoy each other's companionship the more by reason of their rather solitary situation. During the day while Bertha is at school Sanford does not venture far from the house. He has been taught to know the birds, insects and flowers, but he does not enjoy roaming about alone as much as might be expected. In the winter he refuses to play out alone and can only be gotten out of the house on some excuse, like going to meet Bertha.

Sanford is very shy in the presence of adults and will rarely make friends with any man. His mother is somewhat at a loss to account for his timidity, as he has never known any environment other than the present one. She remembers that at about two years he was much frightened at the loud mooing of a cow pastured near by. He is much concerned over any unexplained loud noises, and he very much dislikes storms, although Mrs. Lee has tried to explain to him the nature of electrical storms. Since last fall Sanford has objected to having his door shut at night. This grew up through having it open during the summer, but he understands why it must be closed in the winter.

Sanford is rarely disobedient and has a very amiable disposition with no inclination to sulk. His punishments usually take the form of isolation or sharp spanking of the hands. Sanford has shown some difficulties about eating. At the time of his intestinal trouble, he vomited everything he ate. Four months later, whooping cough interfered with his eating habits and his mother dates his problems from that time. He refuses no one food but he eats extremely slowly and has difficulty with solid foods, chews meat for a long time, and even then cannot swallow it. Bertha adds somewhat to the problem as she is beginning to raise objections to certain foods. Sanford finds talking and listening to his sister much more attractive than eating. Mrs. Lee has tried to avoid making an emotional situation of meal time although she has been somewhat inclined toward over-anxiety owing to her fear of losing him as a baby.

CASES 39 AND 88. STANTON COBB   FOUR YEARS AND TWO MONTHS
JESSICA COBB   SIX YEARS AND FIVE MONTHS
Fears. Feeding problem. Teasing. Temper tantrums.

Home Conditions.—Jessica and Stanton live with their parents in a pleasant, comfortably furnished house in an outlying residential section of a fairly large city. Mr. Cobb is a rising young attorney, who seldom becomes excited and is quiet and consistent in handling the children. Mrs. Cobb is an alert woman, much interested in the scientific aspects of child-training. Most of the discipline falls upon her shoulders altho Mr. Cobb often takes the children off for an afternoon when he has a free day.

Developmental History.—For the first six months of her life, Jessica was very colicky, though in every other way she was regarded as "good." At the end of her first year, she weighed eighteen pounds, but she then began to develop rapidly and is now both tall and heavy for her age. Jessica has always had remarkably good motor control. At the age of two, she delighted in climbing to the top of a newel post and standing there unsupported. At the age of three and a half she used a revolving clothes rack five or six feet above the ground as a merry-go-round while she hung from her knees. At six months, she was already using several words, but at eight months, she started to walk and immediately lost all interest in language and did not resume talking until she was nearly a year old. From that time on, her speech development was very rapid. Both children have a definite tendency toward croup. Jessica has also had frequent colds, measles at the age of three, whooping cough at five, chicken pox at six, and she had her tonsils and adenoids removed at three years. She is at present in good physical condition except for some sinus trouble which has persisted since the attack of measles. She has an IQ of 157.

Except for his tendency to croup, Stanton gave no trouble as a baby. He walked and talked at about a year. He crept very rapidly and this may account for the fact that he was slower than his sister in walking. He weighed eighteen pounds when he was a year old, but for more than a year now has been up to the average for his age. He had whooping-cough at three and a half, and chicken pox at four. He is now in good physical condition except for much enlarged tonsils which are to be removed within the next few weeks. Stanton has an IQ of 142.

History of Adjustments.—Neither child has shown any tendency to enuresis and correct toilet habits were established in both early and easily. Jessica was somewhat finicky about her food till she was three years old. Since then she has gradually acquired more appetite and has relinquished many of her dislikes for particular foods. She has always been fond of all vegetables. Her greatest dislike has been for oatmeal, and this may have been due to too little variation in the cereal. In the case of Stanton the situation has been almost the reverse. Until he was about two and a half, he ate everything, and was considered a model. But since that time he has developed into an eating problem. He is now very fond of some few things, such as meat, bread, raisins, apples, oranges, potatoes and spinach. His greatest dislikes are for carrots, cauliflower, and beans. When the eating problem first arose, Mrs. Cobb began telling Stanton stories about the food he was eating. For example, she would tell him about the growth, drying and shipping of prunes, and then would go on to the process of cooking them and how they were now slipping down his throat. For a considerable time, this method aroused sufficient interest, or at least distracted the boy's attention from his meal enough to get the food into him without protest; but after a time the efficacy diminished so much that other methods had to be tried. Urging has been ineffective. Once or twice the parents have made a definite issue of the meal, and refused to let the child leave the table, or go out to play, etc., until the meal was eaten. This method has a beneficial effect on the next few meals but has had no lasting consequences. Stanton seems, however, under one method or another, to be gradually outgrowing his unfavorable eating habits, and to be eating more of the proper foods. The parents have been unable to account for the onset of this eating problem, and it is definitely not copied from any other member of the family, since all the rest of the family like the foods which Stanton rejects. Both children like to take cod-liver-oil and even ask for it when Mrs. Cobb forgets it.

The sleeping habits of the brother and sister are much alike. Both dropped their naps before they were three, and both of them are extremely restless and wakeful at night if they happen to fall asleep during the day. Both go to sleep quickly at night and neither has had night-terrors although Jessica had frequent bad dreams when she was three. In the matter of fears, however, the two children are quite different. At the age of six weeks, Jessica was showing marked fear of loud noises and of being dropped. All during her third and fourth years she had a feeling of terror toward death, in spite of all the calming influences her parents could exert. Finally at about four and one half she told a neighbor: "When my mother is old, she will die; I'll be about eighteen years old then." From the lightness of the tone it was evident that she had passed her "fear stage," and it has never returned. She also at one time developed an intense fear of dogs which finally cleared up when she went to school and found many of the other children playing with dogs, and all fond of them. Stanton, on the other hand, has shown practically no fear in his entire life. In spite of the fact that he was seriously bitten by a dog at the age of two, he has never feared them, and his constant companion is a little toy dog four or five inches long. This dog is always brought to the table, taken to bed with him and so on. The child seems to be very brave about everything, does not give in to pain and apparently has no physical fear.

A few years ago, Jessica showed a mild tendency toward temper-tantrums, but under the policy of ignoring them, they entirely disappeared, although, of course, she occasionally becomes provoked and cross. Stanton has developed into quite a tease. He has always been strong, and this strength in addition to his disregard of pain and his fearlessness has made him one of the dominant children in the neighborhood. Jessica and the other playmates give up to him in almost all of his desires. Their parents have tried to urge Jessica to fight back when Stanton attacks her, but unless she is extremely irritated and acts upon the impulse of the moment, she continues to let him have his own way. When Stanton occasionally does strike opposition in the other children, he is apt to throw a temper-tantrum, but these have been consistently ignored by the adults of the family, and they are gradually disappearing. Stanton's teasing seems to be a method of exhibiting his physical superiority, and no method has been found yet which stops the teasing for more than a short time. When he pinches, if he is pinched in return, he stops that, but returns with some other method of irritation.

CASE 40. RAYMOND SIEHL   FOUR YEARS AND TWO MONTHS
                    No particular problem.

Home Situation.—Mr. Siehl is a foreman in a manufacturing plant and the family live in a second floor apartment in a fairly good neighborhood. Mr. Siehl enjoys Raymond and his seven-year old brother greatly and spends considerable time with them on Saturday afternoons and Sundays. Because he is a bit inclined to tease the boys in fun they are sometimes uncertain whether or not their father is in earnest, and obey him less promptly than they do their mother. Mrs. Siehl is a very intelligent woman who is alert and anxious to have the boys develop and behave properly. For example, when she was asked whether Raymond ever had temper tantrums, she straightened up and replied "I should say not! Do you think I'd stand for that?" She has been rather exhausted the last few months from the care of the older brother during a succession of illnesses and broken bones.

Developmental History.—Raymond was a healthy, contented baby who walked and talked by the age of one year. With the exception of whooping cough at ten months, he has had no contagious diseases. He shows a general diminution in size although neither of his parents is particularly small. His speech is clear and distinct. The family physician has advised the removal of tonsils and adenoids. On the intelligence test Raymond received an IQ of 117.

History of Adjustments.—Raymond is a very attractive, very lively small boy who is exceptionally popular with both children and adults. He shows a decided inclination to draw other children into his play activities, a readiness to participate in activities initiated by others, and is remarkably cooperative, leading or following as the occasion demands. He is so popular that several of the neighbor children have been known to fight for a chance to play with Raymond. Although he quickly shows resentment when other children infringe upon his rights, he is more inclined to withdraw from the play when displeased than he is to resort to forcible methods of control. He has a keen sense of justice when the point is not obscured by his own sense of humor and his delight in teasing. He perseveres until his goal is reached or until an adult requests him to do something else. The only problem which Raymond has shown is smallness of appetite and slowness in eating. However, if given time enough and if he understands that he is expected to eat everything on his plate, he will usually do so.

CASE 41. DAISY PARLIN   FOUR YEARS AND THREE MONTHS
No particular problem.

Home Situation.—The Parlins live in a rather dilapidated house in a fairly good section of the city. Mr. Parlin, who works in a lumber yard, is apparently too easy-going to trouble with such things as broken door-steps and the like. Mrs. Parlin is also very little disturbed by cluttered rooms and yard, and nothing can ever be found without pawing over a great pile of stuff. She is good natured but not particularly intelligent, and seems to have been extremely unobservant and uninterested in the development of Daisy, her nine year old sister and seven and five year old brothers. The children obey their father better than their mother, but neither parent expects, or gets, prompt obedience.

Developmental History.—Daisy walked and talked at about a year, as nearly as her mother can remember. She had whooping-cough at six months and measles at one year. At present although she is somewhat undersized, like all of her father's family, she is well nourished. Her posture is rather poor, and she seems to have more than an average amount of nose and throat trouble. Otherwise her physical examination is negative. On the intelligence test she received an IQ of only 88 but showed good manual dexterity. She is frequently taken for a child of three.

History of Adjustments.—Daisy shows no particular problems. She is not a very hearty eater and is rather finicky about her food. She likes macaroni and potatoes best, but she "doesn't particularly care for pie and cake." When she gets provoked at not getting her own way, she pouts. If Mrs. Parlin ignores her at these times, Daisy will sulk in a corner for a time and then get over it. She is not a particularly active child and tends to be shy and easily embarrassed. She is very easily controlled and is of a good-natured, even temperament. She seems to prefer to play alone, rather than with a group of children. She is more inclined to follow than to lead. When other children infringe upon her rights, she does not fight back or make any attempt to claim her toy, but withdraws and cries softly to herself. Her social behavior seems to be immature and she probably will learn to take her own place when thrown with other children.

Case 42. EMMA NILSON   Four Years and Three Months
Hard to manage. Variable. Clumsy. Hyperkinetic. Negativistic. Stoical in punishment.

Home Situation.—Emma's father is a struggling young physician. He and Mrs. Nilson were married while he was in medical school on the promise of his grandmother to leave him all of her considerable fortune. As long as this grandmother lived, that is until just before the birth of the youngest child, she provided enough money for the Nilsons to live in a fair amount of comfort. When, however, the grandmother died suddenly it was found that she had left no will and there were so many grandchildren that the part of the fortune falling to Dr. Nilson was insufficient for the support of his family for more than one year. The sudden loss of income has tended to make the man worried and irritable. He sees that his practice is steadily increasing, but realizes that it will be a number of years before the income will be adequate for the luxuries he craves. Mrs. Nilson has always had a great interest in music, and spends hours at the piano when, according to the neighbors, she might be better occupied with family mending and cooking. The home is often in a state of turmoil either on account of Mrs. Nilson's preoccupation with music or on account of Dr. Nilson's irritability. Emma has a sister aged six and a brother aged two. Neither of these displays to any marked degree the characteristics which make a problem of Emma.

Developmental History.—Emma was a rather fussy baby, easily upset by excitement or changes in her routine. She walked at thirteen months and talked at about one year. She has had no diseases except bronchitis and an occasional cold. Her physical examination was negative. On the intelligence test she received an IQ of 102. She was exceedingly negativistic at times and gave good cooperation only on the tests that particularly interested her.

History of Adjustments.—Emma has always been an exceedingly hard child to handle and to teach. She was not trained for correct toilet habits until she was two and a half years old. She is variable from day to day. Some days she eats well and without comment; other days she is inattentive and slow. She is very clumsy, not apparently because of poor coordination but because of speed and heedlessness. She is "on the move" practically all of the time and never seems exhausted. She shows considerable negativism at times and when she is not allowed to continue in the activity in which she is engaged she is more apt than not to throw a temper tantrum. Corporal punishment is entirely ineffective. When spanked she refrains from crying and remarks "That didn't hurt." A short period of isolation has proved the most effective method of control. If another child asks for the toy with which Emma is playing, she is seldom willing to relinquish it unless she is overcome by physical force, in which case she stands aloof, showing extreme resentment, or engages in some independent activity. She in general fascinates younger children, and is always conspicuous in a way to intrigue the crowd, dramatic without imaginative content. Everyone can understand the things that Emma does. Her own inventions, which sometimes give her the lead in a group of children, are apt to be the noisy repetitive, contentless activities of a younger child done with the vigor and persistence of her own years.

Suggested Treatment.—The Nilsons should introduce more calm routine into their home. Mrs. Nilson should if possible give up her music during the daytime, and should get the children fed before their father gets home at night. Emma's environment should be kept as simple and as regular as possible.

<small>CASE 43.   LUCY ANNE HATHAWAY FOUR YEARS AND THREE MONTHS</small>
<small>Restless sleep. Poor appetite. Thumb sucking. Fears.</small>
<small>Plays alone.   Whines. Speech problem.</small>

Home Situation.—Lucy Anne lives with her parents, her seven year old sister and baby brother. Mr. Hathaway is a skilled laborer and earns enough to provide a comfortable home. He is very easy going. His wife is sweet and gentle and hates to hurt anyone's feelings. She is cheerful and optimistic ordinarily but frequently becomes impatient and nags the children.

Developmental History.—Lucy Anne is said to have been a good baby. She walked at eleven months and talked at eighteen months. Except for whooping cough at fourteen months and chicken pox within the last year she has always been well. The child is now definitely undernourished. She has enlarged glands and tonsils and breathes through her mouth. In the intelligence test she received an IQ of 91.

History of Adjustments.—The difficulties in this case have shown a gradual development. At present Lucy Anne is a restless sleeper, has a poor appetite, sucks her thumb, is afraid of dogs, whines considerably, tends to play alone even when other children are in the room, and is difficult to manage. Most of all Mrs. Hathaway is worried about her daughter's poor articulation.

Suggested Treatment.—Lucy Anne should begin taking cod liver oil to help build up her general physical condition. Her tonsils should be removed. She should play more with other children and grow less dependent on her mother. Mrs. Hathaway should discontinue her nagging about the child's speech.

Later History.—A month after the removal of her tonsils Lucy Anne is reported as being much improved; her appetite is better, and she is playing more with other children. Her mother is planning to get her into a speech class as soon as possible. Seven months later Mrs. Hathaway reports that Lucy Anne is in kindergarten and is not getting along very well. The younger brother is now adopting some of Lucy Anne's characteristics. Two months later Lucy Anne returned to the clinic. Her speech is much clearer than last year but it is still hard to understand. Mrs. Hathaway thinks that the child is getting along with other children better, but the kindergarten teacher sees no improvement. She is now attending a school which has a daily speech class.

Case 44. ROY McCURDY   Four Years and Four Months

Feeding problem. Temper tantrums. Obstinate. Hyperkinetic.
Stutters. Takes toys apart. Few playmates.

Home Situation.—For several generations the McCurdy family have been known for their uncontrolled violent tempers. Roy's father becomes angry at slight provocation. He is taking some evening courses in business accounting and if he cannot solve a problem he is likely to throw the books violently from his desk, stamp around the room and tear his hair. He has a great deal of energy and restless activity and withal a perseverance that brings him back to conquer the unsolved problem. Between his work as salesman and his evening classes he is too busy to see much of his son. Mrs. McCurdy is underweight and fatigues easily. She is ordinarily good natured but in her efforts to help her husband fit himself for a better position she is overworking and is frequently impatient and provoked with Roy.

Developmental History.—Roy was never a fretful baby and he was never sick but once when at the age of seven months he was suddenly taken violently ill. He recovered before any diagnosis was made. Roy talked at nine months and walked at thirteen months. As soon as he began to form real sentences, Mrs. McCurdy noticed a tendency to stammer. She also noticed at an early age that he was left handed and she tried gently to break him of this by moving his toys into his right hand. Roy had measles at three and his tonsils were removed the same year. He shows a tendency toward nocturnal enuresis and his mother continues to take him up two or three times a night. His physical examination was negative and his mental test gave him an IQ of 113. In this examination he did not stutter. The right hand was used throughout for handling blocks and drawing, though in reaching out to get something he was likely to use his left hand and later transfer the object to his right hand.

History of Adjustments.—Roy persistently refuses to eat vegetables. He minds fairly well and does not run away nor deliberately destroy the belongings of others, but he insists upon taking his toys apart. He seems to have no interest in toys as a means of play, but wants to dismember everything, from mechanical toys to teddy-bears. He has a hasty temper which is aroused whenever he is frustrated. These spells of temper are becoming more frequent and are increasing in severity. Roy is obstinate. He is extremely restless and has great energy. He is not in the least dependent although he is not a leader among other children, and in fact seldom has an opportunity to play with them. Mrs. McCurdy believes that the stammering is due in part at least to the fact that Roy thinks more rapidly than he can speak. It is always when he is excited about something or when he is most enthusiastic and in a hurry to tell something or to draw attention to something that he stammers. She thinks that the frequency of stammering has decreased in the last year.

Suggested Treatment.—If possible Mr. McCurdy must reduce the nervous tension under which he is living. Roy must play more with other children and should spend less time with his parents.

Later History.—Two months later Mrs. McCurdy reports that she has noticed that Roy stammers only when talking to adults. He is less negativistic since she has provided playmates his own age.

Case 45. FLORENCE LEUSCHNER   Four Years and Four Months
Thumb sucking. Sensitive. Craves attention.

Home Situation.—Dr. and Mrs. Lueschner are very ambitious for themselves and for their children. Dr. Lueschner is a rather nervous physician who has a large practice and is popular socially as well as professionally. Mrs. Leuschner is high strung and is suffering from a mild manic-depressive state. Her moods make the children feel insecure and rather anxious as to how they will be treated next. She says she has "four problem children," but she is without doubt exaggerating for every one else regards the four Leuschner children as normal and ordinarily well behaved. There is no real friction in the home and the parents enter into the children's interests in a very satisfactory manner. Florence's brothers and sister are considerably older than she, one fourteen, one twelve and one ten. They are lively, enthusiastic children, who get along well in school.

Developmental History.—Florence has been unusually well. She has developed at the expected rate, has had no serious diseases, and is at present in excellent physical condition. She has an IQ of 123 and during the examination showed good attention and excellent poise.

History of Adjustments.—Florence sleeps quietly and is not fussy about food although she imitates her sister in refusing certain vegetables. She has never been a behavior problem, but the family are anxious to guard against the further development of certain traits. Her mother in particular is distressed to have Florence suck her thumb, to have her so deeply hurt when scolded or criticized that she runs off to hide, and to have her crave attention to such a marked degree.

Suggested Treatment.—Mrs. Leuschner is evidently at the present time somewhat exhausted. She is probably handling the children poorly and causing emotional upsets that are bad for everyone. She must stop trying to make the children live up to such high standards and should let them discontinue such outside activities as dancing school. Florence should be given as much freedom as possible, should be treated as an adult and not constantly talked of as the "baby of the family." Above all Mrs. Leuschner must stop worrying.

Case 46. GUY DAVENPORT   Four Years and Five Months
    No particular problem. Trained for toilet habits unusually early.

Home Situation.—Mrs. Davenport is a normal school graduate. She is even tempered, well controlled, shrewd and farsighted. Mr. Davenport is a manufacturer's salesman with business college training. He is a pleasant, very adaptable man, extremely fond of his children and ready to share their responsibility when he is at home. The parents cooperate well in the management of Guy and Dorothy, the six months old baby. Both are very desirous of making the most of themselves and of their children.

Developmental History.—Guy and Dorothy have both been bottle-fed babies, Guy from the beginning and Dorothy from the age of six weeks. Both were good babies, fairly easy to care for though not sleeping as long at a stretch as the average child. Neither has had any contagious diseases and Guy did not even have a cold until after he was a year old. They are both in excellent physical condition. On the intelligence test, Guy received an IQ of 115.

History of Adjustments.—The main interest which we have in these children is the matter of the ease and quickness with which Mrs. Davenport has been able to establish correct toilet habits in them. From the beginning she kept Guy dry and scrupulously clean. She began to train him for regular bowel movements at the age of two months and shortly after that started to train him for bladder control. He was completely trained by eight months. Her method was as follows. She made a hammock by hanging an old bath-towel rather loosely by the four corners. She then cut a small hole in the bottom of the hammock and inside of two weeks Guy had learned to have a bowel movement every time he was placed in the hammock. In Dorothy's case, Mrs. Davenport began to train for bladder control at the age of six weeks by holding her on a vessel every half hour while she was awake. After two weeks of this, she was warned by her physician that she was encouraging frequent urination and that she might also be making the child nervous by so much handling. Mrs. Davenport then increased the period to two hours and at the age of four months the child was practically trained. Now, at the age of six months, Dorothy wets a diaper about once in three days. She also calls her mother if she wishes to be placed on the toilet chair at some time between the regular periods by grunting if her bowels are about to move and by a little squeal if she wishes to urinate. Guy never wet the bed at night after he was a year old. Dorothy is not yet trained to remain dry during the night.

Mrs. Davenport attributes her success in establishing these habits early to the exercise of great patience. She considers that the results have been worth the effort, but questions whether the nervousness which is sometimes apparent in Guy may not be due to her over-rigorous insistence upon routine. She feels since she has been reading on child training that her tendency is now not to expect so much of Guy as she did formerly. He is a shy child, sensitive, meticulously neat and systematic in his habits. He gets on well with the older children who are his playmates and enjoys Sunday School greatly.

CASE 47. MADELINE STEVENS   FOUR YEARS AND SIX MONTHS

Nervous. Feeding problem. Restless sleeper. Speech defect.
Objects to having curls brushed.

Home Situation.—Madeline's father is at present clerking in a drug store in order to support the family while he studies pharmacy. He seems to be a quiet, stable, superior man, but he is too busy to have any leisure for Madeline and her two brothers, one eight and the other a baby. Mrs. Stevens is much interested in her family and her home but she seems utterly incapable of accomplishing anything. She is an extremely poor housekeeper, is ungoverned and erratic in her movements, flies from one thing to another, and is apparently in a constant state of "letting off steam." She speaks quickly and "talks the arms off" her neighbors or anyone she sees. Her English is poor because she speaks indistinctly with a Scandinavian accent and runs all her words together so that they are almost indistinguishable. She does, however, always have time to answer the children's questions and often takes them for walks or to the park. Her chief method of punishment is spanking.

Developmental History.—Madeline walked and talked soon after she was a year old and was in general a good baby. She had a convulsion when she was two, has had chicken-pox and measles and about a year ago had her tonsils removed. At present her physical condition is poor, she shows moderate malnutrition and lacks color. On the intelligence test she received an IQ of 117.

History of Adjustments.—Madeline has a poor appetite. Her mother offers her vegetables only once or twice a week but she refuses them even then. She is nervous, a restless sleeper and has nocturnal enuresis occasionally. She has no playmates her own age and seldom plays out-of-doors. Madeline is more difficult to manage than her eight year old brother and at times she is "spunky." She objects violently when her curls are brushed. She speaks very indistinctly.

Suggested Treatment.—Madeline should eat vegetables every day. She should be given a scrap-book in which to record her meals. (This suggestion was made as much for Mrs. Stevens' benefit as for Madeline's, since the clinic felt that Mrs. Stevens was so undependable that she might—wholly unintentionally—forget the vegetables for several successive days.) Madeline should be punished by isolation or some sort of deprivation, rather than by spanking. She should get plenty of sleep and should be taken up once during the night. Her curls might be cut if they seem to be a real source of irritation.

Later History.—Two months later Mrs. Stevens reports that at first Madeline's appetite improved for a while but lately (perhaps on account of a great deal of candy during the Christmas holidays), she had eaten very little. Her general condition is now fair. Mrs. Stevens must try to speak more slowly and exactly herself in order to set a good example for her daughter. Since the enuresis problem has not entirely cleared up, Madeline should receive only a limited amount of liquids in the late afternoon. Mrs. Stevens seldom has time to write in the scrap-book. Madeline's teeth now need attention. They are decayed and need brushing.

Seven months later Madeline's teeth look very much better since she has been brushing them regularly. She is also speaking much more distinctly, perhaps because she has been visiting an uncle who refused to listen to her unless she spoke plainly. Her appetite is still variable. She is enjoying kindergarten.

Six months later Mr. Stevens has a little more time for his family now and he is working with Madeline on her speech. The results are good although she would probably make still more rapid improvement if she could enter a speech class. Her curls have been cut, she is eating well, and everybody is happier.

Case 48. HUGO SCOTT   Four Years and Six Months
Fatigue. Restless sleep. Nail biting. Fears. Insane mother.
Prefers to play alone.

Home Situation.—The family background of the Scotts is rather unstable; there are several cases of insanity, uncontrollable temper, and so on. Mr. Scott is a day-laborer, said to be a good reliable worker, but lacking in backbone and unduly influenced by his wife. He is at present unemployed. When his first wife died he showed no affection for the children, and was glad to have her relatives take them. He has a violent temper, is cross and irritable with children, is filthy about his person, and used to drink to excess. Hugo's mother was sent to an insane asylum by her first husband eleven years ago, and she was divorced from him some years later. Three other times, once when Hugo was three weeks old, she has spent periods in asylums, and has been classified as a "manic-depressive." She is nervous and irritable at times and quarrels with neighbors almost constantly. She is very suspicious of everyone and fearful of being again confined in a State Hospital. · She has been frequently heard using obscene and vulgar language. She has threatened to kill several of the neighbors and they have had to be escorted to and from home by an officer. As long as Mr. Scott is at home she seems to treat the children at least decently, but in his absence she has been known to knock Hugo down, and to deliberately burn him simply in giving vent to her anger. In addition to Hugo there are an eleven-year old half-sister and a baby brother living with the parents. The family have moved frequently, and the personnel of the family has been constantly changing with now the addition and now the loss of a half-brother or sister. Some months ago the courts removed Hugo from his own home and placed him in a boarding home. This house is very attractive and the child has more advantages than he has ever had before. The boarding mother however is not particularly wise in her attitude toward the child. She talks frequently in his presence about his being a charity case or about his bad behavior, and she threatens to send him from her home if he doesn't act better. She seems more or less unstable herself, is restless and fidgety, says she can't talk over the telephone without crying, and is sure she has severe "heart trouble."

Developmental History.—Hugo walked at about a year and talked a little earlier. At the age of two he had a severe attack of influenza and afterwards had to learn to walk all over again. At three he had measles. At present he is fairly well developed and nourished. He shows many scars on his face, scalp, back and arms, the result of his mother's attacks. His muscular coordination is poor. On the intelligence test he received an IQ of 108.

History of Adjustments.—In the boarding home, Hugo is said to have an enormous appetite and to be ready to eat anything. He fatigues easily. His sleep is apt to be restless and he talks in his sleep if he has played hard the day before. Lately he has been having bad night-mares, and has been crying out that his mother should not take him away. He is neat and tidy about his person and is much interested in his personal appearance. He bites his nails but doesn't suck his thumb, or stutter. There is no trouble with bed wetting if he is given no water in the late afternoon. When he came to live at his present home he seemed to have no conception of play and even now prefers to play alone. Occasionally he joins some active game with other children, but he soon tires and returns to a quiet block construction. He is very systematic about putting away his toys. Hugo refuses to stay outdoors in the fear that his mother will find him and carry him home with her.

Temper tantrums occur at times but they are becoming somewhat less frequent. When first in the boarding home, Hugo was easily frightened. For example he would not relax when he was being carried for fear the boarding mother would drop him as his mother had purposely done at times. He is stubborn and won't respond to any kind of punishment. He pays close attention, is obedient, honest and cheerful and doesn't cry easily.

Suggested Treatment.—Hugo needs a well-regulated regimen of diet, exercise, and rest. An indirect attack should be made upon the child's profound fears. Although he is very fond of his present boarding mother, he would probably make a more rapid gain in self-confidence and self-reliance if he could be placed in an environment which will be conducive to his forgetting his past unhappy experiences, and to forgetting that he is a "charity case." As soon as he is old enough he should be placed in a kindergarten.

CASE 49. PAUL GUTERMAN   FOUR YEARS AND SIX MONTHS
   (see case 15)
CASE 50. EDNA DORSETT   FOUR YEARS AND SEVEN MONTHS
   (see case 4)
CASE 51. NED WORTHINGTON   FOUR YEARS AND NINE MONTHS
Speech defect. Destructive. Slow in learning. Feeling of inferiority.

Home Situation.—Ned lives in a good neighborhood with his
parents and his two sisters, one aged nine who is "nervous and
active," and the other aged six who has a speech defect that is
improving.   Practically all the relatives have had High School
education and none shows any mental or nervous peculiarity except the paternal grandfather who has an ungovernable temper.
Ned's father, who is a life insurance agent, is also quick to show
anger and impatient when things he is doing do not turn out well.
He is rather precise but he lacks firmness and fatigues easily.
He worries a great deal and nags the children when they annoy
him.   Mrs. Worthington is pleasant and friendly though somewhat timid.   She is extremely nervous, easily depressed, complains a great deal and is inclined to over-estimate her own ailments.   She is said to be a "finicky hypochondriac."   She refuses
to go out without her husband and children even though she acknowledges that "the family are together so much they get on
each other's nerves."

Developmental History.—Ned was a fairly good baby who
walked at fifteen months but did not talk till he was three years
old.   He had measles at a year and a half, whooping cough at
two, and scarlet fever at four.   He is now a somewhat undernourished, hyperactive child who gives evidence of early rickets.
He has an IQ of 91.

History of Adjustments.—Mrs. Worthington says that Ned
has always been slow to learn.   It took her a full year to teach
him to use his toilet chair.   She tried spanking and punishments
of all sorts but they were unavailing.   He has been slow in learning to talk and does not speak plainly even yet.   It took nearly a
year to teach him to say "Please excuse me" when leaving the
table and not till he was nearly four could he be taught to keep
out of the street.   Ned is quite destructive, not because he is malicious but on account of awkwardness.   Because he cries and

refuses to listen to explanation, he gets spanked a great deal. Withal he is quite a contented child and seems to feel a certain responsibility for his mother and sisters when he is out with them. In the clinic he showed marked inhibition and restraint and gave the impression that he was conforming entirely to standards and obligations imposed upon him and that he had little opportunity for self-expression. His movements were slow. Comparison with his unusually alert sister has evidently produced a feeling of inferiority which the child tries to compensate by over-cautiousness and timidity.

Suggested Treatment.—Mrs. Worthington should get more recreation herself. She should not try to force Ned up to his more alert sister. He should be sent to kindergarten as soon as possible.

Later History.—Two months later Ned is said to be happier though still somewhat irresponsible. After he had been in kindergarten some weeks, the teacher reported that the boy did not take part in the group work but merely stood and looked on. Mrs. Worthington seems to be sensitive about the child.

CASE 52. JOSEPH STRAND FOUR YEARS AND NINE MONTHS
Stubborn. Slow in dressing. Negativism.
Petted and shown off by many adults.

Home Situation.—The home life of the Strands is happy and congenial. The father is a mechanic. He is fond of Joseph and the baby sister and kind to them though he tends to be nervous and quick tempered. Mrs. Strand is an attractive little woman who is if anything over-anxious about the children.

Developmental History.—Joseph was a colicky baby who walked at eleven and talked at eighteen months. He had whooping cough at three years and chicken pox at five. He has never had a good appetite but is nevertheless well developed and nourished. In the clinic he refused to talk enough to get a satisfactory intelligence test but he probably would grade near the average for his age.

History of Adjustments.—When he was a baby Joseph was frequently surrounded by proud relatives who petted and cajoled him so much that Mrs. Strand presently began to notice a tendency in the child to "shut up like a clam whenever anyone was about." At present Joseph is very stubborn, shows a definite negativism and tends to reject flatly any suggestion which is made to him. He refuses to eat vegetables and then runs to his grandparents who live down stairs for sweet lunches between meals. He will accept no assistance in dressing but is so slow and does so many other things at the same time that he sometimes is not completely clothed before afternoon. Lately Joseph has taken the notion not to have a bowel movement without undressing completely.

Suggested Treatment.—The mother must be more firm. The family should if possible move further away from the grandparents and Joseph should be sent to kindergarten as soon as possible.

Later History.—After four months Joseph is reported as dressing somewhat more quickly since his mother has been more firm. With the approach of winter Mrs. Strand refused to allow him to undress for his bowel movement for fear he would catch cold and it is rather amusing to note that her firmness was followed by immediate compliance on the part of the child. Joseph is now in kindergarten. For the first six or eight weeks there he showed no interest in the children or their activities, but he is gradually responding more and more and the teacher says he is "good but shy and quiet." The situation at home has been improving also. Mrs. Strand has Joseph alone more and is no longer expecting him to respond to all the adults who come in.

CASE 53. HOWARD HEPBURN   FOUR YEARS AND TEN MONTHS
Mild fear. Tendency toward bullying.

Home Situation.—The Hepburns live in a pleasant bungalow in a good residential section of the city. Mr. Hepburn is head of a large department in a manufacturing concern and provides many luxuries for the family. He is a very intelligent man with an excellent disposition. He is devoted to Howard and his year old sister, but is at the same time firm with them and they obey him promptly and pleasantly. Mrs. Hepburn was a teacher before her marriage and is greatly interested in the development and training of the children. She seems to be a remarkably good disciplinarian, and the atmosphere of the home is genial.

Developmental History.—Howard was a very good baby, never had colic and was seldom fussy. He walked at fifteen months and talked at about a year. He has had light cases of whooping cough and chicken pox, but no other contagious diseases. He is at present very well developed and nourished and in excellent physical condition. He has an IQ of 125.

History of Adjustments.—There has never been any trouble with enuresis. At one time. Mrs. Hepburn tried taking Howard to the toilet during the night, but she found this woke him up so much that he had difficulty in getting to sleep afterwards, so she abandoned the plan, and within a few months Howard had trained himself to stay dry through the whole night. He has been no feeding problem at all until the last year. The baby sister was rather frail and sickly for some months and occupied her mother's entire time. This let the care of Howard fall upon a maid who worships him and she spoiled him by giving him dessert before the vegetables were eaten. Another trouble arises in the summertime when the boy doesn't want to spend enough time away from play to finish his meal. Now that the sister is better and Mrs. Hepburn is with Howard more, the little feeding difficulty is clearing up quickly. One rule of the house is that no one, whether child, father, maid, or visiting aunt is allowed to say he dislikes any food. The food provided is eaten by everyone without unfavorable comment. Howard sleeps quietly without any indication of terrors or bad dreams. He has shown a slight fear of dogs since he was bitten in the arm two years ago, but this is not expressed by any reaction more violent than shrinking away. Mr. Hepburn is working on this fear by taking care to pat and talk to dogs when walking with Howard. When the baby sister was born, Howard was evidently jealous. He would go off and sit in a chair with a woe-begone expression whenever his mother picked the baby up, and he once said "I wish I was a little baby so you would hold me." The parents have conquered this attitude by appealing to his pride in being a big boy. Howard occasionally displays temper by sulking, never by tantrums. Mr. Hepburn punishes Howard by depriving him of something, though

Howard adores his father so much that there is usually no cause for punishment when they are together. One of the worst things that can happen to the boy is to feel that his father disapproves of him. Howard has some little difficulty in playing with other children. There are none of his exact age in the neighborhood, and the older ones bully him, and he then retaliates by bullying the younger boys. Howard has been attending Sunday School this winter and enjoying it greatly. He apparently makes a good social adjustment there.

CASE 54. MARGARET TAYLOR   FOUR YEARS AND TEN MONTHS
Feeding problem. Irritable. Chews hair. Temper tantrums.
Sucks thumb. Speech defect. Disobedient. Feeble minded.

Home Situation.—The Taylor family live in a two room shanty and seem not particularly dissatisfied with their condition. The father is a day laborer. He is attached to Margaret and her two year old sister, but his judgment in regard to them seems to lack comprehension and insight. The mother is slack, contented and self-satisfied. She cries easily. Neither parent believes in punishment and both give in to Margaret's tantrums.

Developmental History.—Margaret was a fussy, fretful baby and has never been well and strong. She has had measles and has abcesses in her ears every winter. Enuresis persisted till two or three months ago. At present she is much underweight and generally inferior physically. She is also inferior intellectually with an IQ of 51. All her reactions are infantile.

History of Adjustments.—As soon as Margaret's hair was long enough to grasp, she began to pull it out and chew it, even swallowing some at times. She is highly irritable, a finicky eater, and has frequent temper tantrums. She pays no attention to commands. Thumb sucking has been present since an early age. The child speaks very indistinctly, with practically nothing but grunts and mumbles and she flies into a rage if not understood. Her training has always been inadequate and inconsistent and her objectionable habits have been strengthened by constant scolding, nagging, punishment and threatening.

Suggested Treatment and Results.—When her parents were told that Margaret was inferior physically and intellectually, they objected strenuously, declaring that she is a "mighty bright little girl." Suggestions as to firmer and more consistent discipline were likewise discarded and remarks about the advantages of a school for the feeble-minded fell upon deaf ears.

Case 55. PALMER STODDARD   Four Years and Ten Months
Quarrelsome. Bully. Selfish. Defies authority. Hyperkinetic. Impulsive. Destructive. Feeding problem. Bedwetting. Too high standards.

Home Situation.—Palmer's father is a very successful business man who would have finished a college course if he had not had an unusual offer to accompany an uncle on a business trip to South America. On his return he entered the uncle's wholesale house and is now manager. As a child Mr. Stoddard is said to have shown many reactions like those exhibited by Palmer, but he now is a very popular man, very active, always on the go, and exacting, though not quick tempered. Mrs. Stoddard is fussy and particular about her housekeeping, her children and herself. She is nervous and loses patience easily. Palmer has two brothers, one age eight, the other two, and a baby sister. The eight year old brother appears to be an unusually gifted child. His IQ is 135 and he has never shown any problems. Parents as well as neighbors and friends adore him. The home life is in general harmonious, though the parents confess that they are probably too severe and too quick in their punishment. Mrs. Stoddard says with a little laugh that Palmer is "impossible, beyond hope," and that she is very free in telling him that she can't handle him and that his father will be interviewed when he gets home, etc. Palmer is not at all disturbed by his mother's punishments and very little by those of his father. Mr. and Mrs. Stoddard both compare Palmer unfavorably with his older brother.

Developmental History.—Palmer walked and talked before he was a year old. He was a restless sleeper as a baby, but he sleeps quietly now. He had whooping cough at one year, measles at two, and had his tonsils removed at three. At the present time, he is well developed and well nourished, though slightly underweight. On the intelligence tests he received an IQ of 98. During the examination he was obedient and docile. He showed a slight speech defect, which seemed to be largely oral inactivity, an infantile type of speech.

History of Adjustments.—From the age of two Palmer has been a behavior problem. He wets the bed not only at night but also during his afternoon nap. He seems now to be more or less of a bully. He is so rough and strenuous that even older boys are afraid of him. He takes great delight in athletic stunts. One of his uncles has trained him and with him given exhibitions before the family and a few friends. Palmer has been so much in his glory at these times that Mr. Stoddard has persuaded the uncle to confine their athletics to the attic and to invite no spectators. Palmer is very selfish, helps himself freely to toys of others and if he strikes opposition, starts a fight. He defies authority, and when punished never shows any emotion save that afterward he sits by himself and pouts till his father makes him laugh by tickling him. His chief offense in his mother's eyes is that he absolutely ignores all requests and orders. In fact he is most likely to do just the opposite thing. He is never still a moment, "moves like a streak of lightning." He is very impulsive and his parents never know when the leg of a chair may be sawed off, or any of their personal property may be used in his play. He destroys his own toys "with one bang." He starts quarrels on the least provocation, knocks the other children down, and does things to "get his brother's goat." Palmer seems to take more delight in annoying his brother than in any other activity except his athletic stunts. When forced to eat, he gags and regurgitates the food. Mrs. Stoddard claims that at one time they attempted to starve him into eating, but after three days he still failed to display any appetite. Mr. Stoddard can sometimes get things done by ordering Palmer to do just the opposite.

Suggested Treatment.—The parents must understand that Palmer is not a superior child and they must cease trying to hold him up to the achievements of his brilliant older brother. The discipline should be consistent and Mrs. Stoddard must not try to establish more than one habit in the child at a time. It is evident that Palmer's mother lacks the poise and control necessary for training a difficult child. He has been unwisely treated from birth, spoiled by his father, and handled erratically by his mother. At the present time he never believes what his mother says to him. It would therefore be a good scheme to send Palmer to a kindergarten and so keep him away from his mother as much as possible. Mr. and Mrs. Stoddard were given pamphlets on enuresis with the suggestion that they select the treatment which seems best suited to Palmer's case.

Later History.—After two months Mrs. Stoddard reported that when Palmer's father offered him a prize if he would keep his bed dry for three nights, there was no enuresis but as soon as he received the prize the enuresis began again. They have tried giving him stars on a chart for dry nights but without avail. His mother says she can't deny him liquids in the late afternoon because he coaxes and is so appealing. The parents apparently fail to understand the difference in mental ability between Palmer and his older brother and they refuse to believe that Palmer's behavior is the result of an unsatisfactory competition with him.

After another month the kindergarten teacher reported that Palmer's general conduct and adaptation were excellent but that one day his mother visited school and he immediately began jumping around and disregarding orders. Mrs. Stoddard is discouraged about the enuresis.

Case 56. TOM ORTH   Four Years and Ten Months
Feeding problem. Speech defect, Negativistic. Dependent upon mother.
Nervous mother.

Home Situation.—Tom's father is a vigorous, enthusiastic engineer whose work in building new railroads sometimes takes him away from home for two or three months at a time. At other times he may be at home for several consecutive weeks. He is extravagant, indulgent and extremely fond of his children. Mrs. Orth comes from a family of "chronic worriers." She worries for fear the children will annoy the neighbors, and worries about the family finances. She is often cross, irritable and nagging. She refuses to share the care of the children with anyone else and so is their almost constant companion. Mrs. Orth says she is anxious to do what is best for the children but is evidently well satisfied with what she has accomplished. She is particularly proud of her seventeen year old son, who is a "wonderful boy," although he has an IQ of only 95. The only daughter, who is six years old, has a slight speech defect and is said to be "nervous." There are neighbor children of Tom's age.

Developmental History.—As a baby Tom was perfectly well. He walked at eleven months and talked at one year. Except for scarlet fever at three, he has had no serious diseases. At the present time his physical examination is negative. He has an IQ of 117.

History of Adjustments.—Mrs. Orth thinks Tom eats too little. He does not rebel when urged to eat, but merely takes a spoonful or two and says he is full. He shows a marked tendency to cling to his mother. She, in turn, seems a bit flattered by such behavior. About six months ago Tom developed the habit of pausing before each word or phrase he speaks and he is substituting "s" for "f". This gives the impression of baby-talk. In the clinic the child was very negativistic. This was taken to be probably due to the ineffectual nagging of a nervous and poorly poised mother.

Suggested Treatment.—Mr. Orth should have more interest and influence in the home and Mrs. Orth less. She should enter into more social activities and allow the children to play away from home fairly frequently. She must also encourage independence in Tom, insist upon his dressing himself, etc.

Later History.—Two months later conditions had improved somewhat especially since Mr. Orth has been trying to insist upon greater independence for Tom.

CASE 57. DAVID ZINMANN   FOUR YEARS AND ELEVEN MONTHS
Destructive. Teasing. Cruel. Hyperkinetic. Emotionally unstable.
Neighborhood pest. Swears.

Home Situation.—The Zinmanns live in a neighborhood of working people. Mr. Zinmann is a wall-paperer and is a calm man who gets on well with David and his two year old sister. Mrs. Zinmann has a profound respect for her husband and for his views on child training, but she seems unable to carry out his ideas. She seems to be a typical "clinging vine." She means well but is absolutely inadequate and lacking in force. She laughs at the children's misdemeanors most of the time but occasionally loses her temper.

Developmental History.—For the first three months of his life David was colicky but after that seemed "quite a good baby" although he was restless and active. He walked at eleven months and talked at thirteen months. He did not acquire perfect bladder control before the age of three. He has had no serious diseases. David's physical examination was negative. On his first intelligence test he received an IQ of 80 but when retested nine months later, it was 90. On this second examination he was more cooperative and not so restless. His speech is infantile.

History of Adjustments.—David's appetite is poor and he is fussy about his food. He can't sit still long enough to be read to. Whenever David goes into a crowd of boys, there is a fight; he is apt to be rough with the younger children and he is known as the "neighborhood pest." For the past year he has been bringing home things that do not belong to him, wagons, kiddie kars, and the like. When asked where he got them he says he doesn't know, but he takes them to their owner when his mother insists. He is so destructive that Mrs. Zinmann is always afraid he will smash the toy before he gets it returned. David swears fluently though his father never does. His mother is somewhat amused at this but usually corrects him and talks to him at length about it. David teases his little sister unmercifully and is delighted when she reacts violently. He shows considerable cruelty and tortures neighborhood cats. No matter how seriously he is punished, he acts the same way next day. He puts the blame on other children. Mrs. Zinmann says the boy is totally irresponsible and cannot be trusted to do anything. He is hyperkinetic, likes to show off and blusters around before other children. Many of his reactions are infantile and emotional instability is marked. When he threw a temper tantrum in the clinic, his mother gave evidence of total inability to cope with the situation.

Suggested Treatment.—Mrs. Zinmann should give David more responsibility, a little at a time. He should be required to play in his own yard and with other children if they will come. He should be kept fairly strictly to a routine and should go to kindergarten as soon as possible.

Later History.—Four months later his mother reports that David's improvement has been remarkable. She sees now that she was wrong in being impatient. He now plays well with his sister, is learning to dress himself, eats more vegetables, and has not destroyed anything since his father gave him a severe scolding for breaking a kitchen window. Two months later his kindergarten teacher was interviewed. She said that in David's first two weeks with her, his behavior was so extraordinary that she put forth considerable effort on him. He is now her "pride and joy, contented, interested and playing well with other children." The teacher also said that the boy showed "more marked anxiety and more marked lack of faith in the word of adults than any child she had ever seen." After another seven months, the report is that David's disagreeable conduct is now directed solely at his mother who persists in her nagging.

CASE 58. ROBERTA TEAL   FIVE YEARS AND NO MONTHS
    Shy. Lazy. Stubborn. Feeding problem. Over-solicitous mother.

Home Situation.—Roberta comes from stable American stock on both sides of the family and apparently has no relatives exhibiting any nervous or mental disease. Her maternal grandmother is very devoted to the child and if it were not for Roberta's mother, would "spoil her to death and indulge her in every possible way." The Teals live in an attractive two-story house in a good neighborhood. They entertain a good deal informally and Roberta is often allowed to join the group. Mr. Teal is a well-to-do chemist. He is usually patient and considerate with his daughter but he becomes so disturbed about her refusal to eat, and the way she plays with her food that the entire family are exhausted at the end of the evening meal. Mrs. Teal explains that her husband fatigues easily, coming home both mentally and physically exhausted, and is apt to be a bit irritable until he gets his own dinner and has had a little rest. Mrs. Teal gives the impression of a rather phlegmatic sort of person, easy-going and as patient as Job. She is much wrapped up in Roberta, and willing to spend any amount of time in the effort to improve the child's eating.

Developmental History.—Roberta has always been healthy. Her tonsils were removed at the age of three, but she has had no contagious diseases. She began to talk and walk by eighteen months. At present she is very well developed and nourished, but she shows slight signs of hypothyroidism. On the intelligence tests she received an IQ of 108.

History of Adjustments.—Roberta is exceedingly shy and timid with strangers, but after she feels acquainted she is friendly and apt to monopolize the attention of anyone. She sleeps soundly, and gives no indications of bad dreams. She sucked her thumb until she was about two and a half, but her mother broke her of the habit by pinning long stockings over her arms. She has had no fears or terrors. There has been no enuresis problem. At the age of four Roberta was sent to a private kindergarten. There she plays nicely with the other children, and enters into their games although she shows little initiative or leadership. She likes to be read to and to help with little household tasks. She is energetic and lively about her play, but lazy and stubborn about other things. For example one day she sat at the table for two hours before she was willing to say "Excuse me." She has a vivid imagination and sings and talks to herself before going to sleep. She is interested and alert, and quite normal in all her reactions except eating.

Roberta has never had a good appetite. Her feeding problem started at about the time she should have begun to feed herself. At this time Mrs. Teal was not well herself and was more irritable than usual. In the morning the mother feels that she must persevere in getting something into Roberta before she starts out for the day, and she has therefore invented all sorts of games to help the food down. They play, for example, that each spoonful of cereal is a person who wants to get into Roberta's little red house (her mouth) etc. Milk has been almost as difficult to get into the child although her mother has used all the devices which she heard of or could invent. She has provided straws, pasted pictures on the bottom of the outside of the glass, and so on, but Roberta has never given the slightest indication that she would be willing to feed herself. Mrs. Teal wanted Roberta to go to kindergarten and she has felt it necessary to get breakfast into her before she starts off. Occasionally at noon, Roberta becomes interested in some particular food and eats it without urging, but she usually refuses to eat more than a bite or two unless she is coaxed and cajoled. If left by herself to finish a meal, she may take two hours to get it eaten. Mrs. Teal has tried other methods, she has cut sandwiches into fancy shapes and put raisins in for eyes, has offered bribes, has attempted to interest the child in pictures of foods, and so on, but all methods have been without avail and every meal ends by the mother's feeding the child. Other children have been invited in for meals and Roberta has been allowed almost to starve herself for three days, but the feeding problem has continued. The only things she really likes are mayonnaise, cheese, and olives. Occasionally she seems fond of custard and will eat her dinner fairly rapidly in order to obtain the dessert, but the next day custard will return to disfavor. Within the last six months Roberta has cultivated the art of choking, gagging, and even vomiting when forced to eat food she dislikes. The last treatment tried was to leave Roberta for a period of three weeks in the charge of a practical nurse, but when the family returned, the nurse was "almost crazy" because of the child's refusal to eat.

Suggested Treatment.—In the clinic it was pretty clear that much of Roberta's activity was directed toward gaining her mother's attention. The physician prescribed for the thyroid condition. Mrs. Teal was advised to withdraw as much as possible from the child's activities, and to read several of the recommended books on child training.

Later History.—Two months later Roberta is reported as eating in a normal fashion for the first time in her life, and a year and a half later, Mrs. Teal says that there are now very infrequent recurrences of the eating problem. The situation has apparently been improved by the arrival of a baby brother, now three months old.

CASE 59. JAMES HOLDEN   FIVE YEARS AND NO MONTHS
     (see case 13)

CASE 60. LILLIAN LAITE   FIVE YEARS AND ONE MONTH
                    Listless. Plays alone.

Home Situation.—Mr. and Mrs. Laite were divorced some months previous to the birth of Lillian and her twin brother. Another daughter, who was a year old at that time, has been taken to live with her grandparents in a small town and she seldom sees her mother and siblings. Mr. Laite contributes about twenty-five dollars a month toward the family expenses. Mrs. Laite and the twins are living in a boarding-house where the mother is the cook. She is a pleasant, even-tempered woman, sincerely interested in the well-being of her children and struggling to bring them up well in spite of lack of education, a broken home, and so forth. In the boarding-house there are two other mothers and several children between the ages of one and three. The atmosphere of the home is pleasant and the employer of Mrs. Laite is kind and considerate of the children.

Developmental History.—Both Lillian and her twin were good babies. The twin walked at thirteen months, Lillian at seventeen months. Lillian talked at twelve months. She had chicken-pox at eleven months, small-pox at twelve months, measles at twenty months, and mumps at four years. At present Lillian's physical examination is practically negative except for moderately enlarged tonsils and markedly decayed teeth.

History of Adjustments.—Lillian has a good appetite and is very fond of vegetables. Her pronunciation is suggestive of baby-talk and she is timid. There have been no temper tantrums and in general she is an easy child to manage, thus differing from her twin. She sleeps soundly in the bed with her mother and her twin. She does not play well with other children. Instead of entering into their games, she stands aside and watches them. In all her actions she shows a marked listlessness.

Suggested Treatment.—Lillian should be taken to a dentist at once to have her teeth filled or extracted. She should be praised, encouraged, and be given more self-confidence. She should be provided with playmates of her own age and should be encouraged to play with them. She should sleep alone. Lillian should be sent to kindergarten as soon as the new term starts.

Later History.—A month later Mrs. Laite reports that Lillian is now through her long siege at the dentist's. She looks much better, has a rosy color now, an appetite even better than formerly, and is much more happy and active. She is now in kindergarten and behaves well though she does not like it particularly. This, her mother thinks, is probably because the place and the children are still strange to her and she does not feel acquainted yet.

CASE 61. BLANCHE KAVANAUGH   FIVE YEARS AND ONE MONTH

Spoiled. Hyperkinetic. Sleeping problem. Feeding problem.
Night terrors. Thumbsucking. Enuresis. Negativistic.
Incapable mother.

Home Situation.—The Kavanaughs live in a rather untidy flat over a grocery store. Mr. Kavanaugh is a plumber. He considers his wife quite stupid in her attitude toward the children and much too lenient. Mrs. Kavanaugh is rather manic and extremely excitable and she keeps the atmosphere at the home keyed high. She seems to have little idea of discipline, partly because the children are so appealing and partly because of their father's rather harsh attitude. An aunt reports that Blanche has been "humored to the limit." Blanche has two older brothers, one twelve and one ten.

Developmental History.—Blanche was a good baby and gave no trouble her first two years. She walked and talked at about fifteen months. At two years she had scarlet fever and at four pneumonia. At present her physical condition is good save for the fact that she is somewhat underweight and has adenoids and enlarged tonsils. She has an IQ of 97.

History of Adjustments.—Since she had scarlet fever Blanche has become more and more spoiled. She is extremely over-active, is a restless sleeper, has night terrors, eats poorly, sucks her thumb, is hard to manage, has mild temper tantrums, and wets her clothes frequently during the day when she forgets to come in from play. In the clinic Blanche was extremely negativistic and objected to things suddenly, unexpectedly.

Suggested Treatment.—Blanche needs cod-liver oil and needs to eat more. Mrs. Kavanaugh must be more firm and must ignore the temper tantrums.

Later History.—Two months later Blanche is in kindergarten and is enjoying it greatly. Ignoring has helped the tantrums. For example, the other day Blanche screamed for two hours while her mother paid no attention. Finally the child asked "Don't you hate to hear me scream?" When Mrs. Kavanaugh answered "No, I like it" Blanche promptly stopped. Four months later the report is that Blanche's improvement was only temporary. She is definitely not up to the other kindergarten children and her mother seems entirely unable to handle her.

CASE 62. EMIL SCHRAM   FIVE YEARS AND TWO MONTHS
                    Periodic vomiting.

Home Situation.—The Schrams live in a single house in a fairly good neighborhood. Mr. Schram is a mechanic in a garage. He is a very gentle man, and is fond of the children, who mind him well. He leaves all the discipline to his wife as he is amused at their faults and is inclined to be lax. It is true, however, that the children are so fond of him that they rarely present problems when with him. He is so friendly and companionable that if he is laid off in a slack time of work, he often cares for them two or three days at a time while their mother goes away for a change. Mrs. Schram, though nervous, is amiable. She has very good control of her children, is forceful, and very firm with the determination to carry out what she undertakes. The family are congenial, and happy, although Mrs. Schram has some difficulty in controlling her temper. Emil has a sister of three, said to be stubborn at times, and a brother of two who likes to have his own way.

Developmental History.—Emil was a colicky baby for three or four months, but was well after that. He walked at fourteen months, and talked at seventeen months. He had acquired bowel and bladder control by twenty-two months. He had chicken pox at the age of four and has always had many colds. His physical examination at present shows a fair nutrition, enlarged and infected tonsils, and enlarged cervical glands. He has attacks of vomiting, usually during the night about once in two months for which no cause has been determined.

History of Adjustments.—Emil has never been a behavior problem, and was brought to the clinic merely on account of the recurrent vomiting. He sleeps quietly, apparently without dreams or terrors. His appetite is good and he is not finicky about his food. He has many playmates who are devoted to him, is socially very responsive and is apparently liked by every one with whom he comes in contact.

Suggested Treatment.—Emil's tonsils and adenoids should be removed as soon as possible.

Later History.—Emil's tonsils were taken out, and a month later he was said to be enjoying kindergarten immensely. He is now staying for a time with his grandmother a block or two from his own home. Mrs. Schram found that he was constantly disturbed by the younger children interfering with his favorite occupations of cutting and pasting and this was keeping him in a state of constant irritation. He is enjoying his visit with the grandmother extremely, and even objects to returning to his own home for an afternoon, for fear he will have to remain there. It is apparently not that he is spoiled by his grandmother but that he enjoys the quietness and freedom from interruption. After another month Emil was taken home again, to prevent his becoming too completely separated from his own family. After a difficult day or two, he and the younger children are getting along well together. There have been two vomiting attacks since the first visit to the clinic. The physician advised Mrs. Schram to avoid mentioning the vomiting before Emil. Two months later the vomiting still occurs occasionally and the physician recommended trying baking soda. After another two months Mrs. Schram reported that there had been no recurrence of the vomiting, but she didn't know whether it had stopped because the boy was older, or because he had had the soda, or because he had recently been taking malted milk.

CASE 63.   MINERVA OTIS   FIVE YEARS AND TWO MONTHS
Hyperkinetic.   Stoical in punishment.   Indifferent.
Controlled by many adults.

Home Situation.—Last year Mr. Otis followed the example of his father and deserted his family. He was extravagant and generous toward his friends, but usually indifferent toward Minerva and the baby brother, whom he regarded as "inevitable nuisances." Mrs. Otis is temperamentally restless like Minerva. She now regrets that she divorced her husband, is still very fond of him and never makes harsh statements about him to the children. Mrs. Otis and the two children are living with the maternal grandparents and uncle. The mother has gone back to her stenographic work. It is a family where each ordinarily goes his own way without consulting the others, but when they come together, there are repeated small annoyances and continual strain. The grandmother cannot forget that Mrs. Otis' marriage was an elopement and frequently reminds her that the relatives had always predicted disastrous consequences. The adults in the family never agree on the treatment of the children and each considers the methods employed by the others as entirely ineffectual.

Developmental History.—Minerva was never ill or fussy or fretful. She walked and talked by the time she was a year old. Minerva is at present well developed and nourished. On the intelligence tests she received an IQ of 97, was very quiet and laughed nervously at her failures. She seemed over-sensitive and over-responsive to stimuli.

History of Adjustments.—Minerva is extremely energetic, moves, wiggles and jumps about every second. She has always slept well, except for occasional dreams of ogres, giants, etc. She has now learned to ask for only mildly pleasant stories at night. Her appetite is poor and she eats only what her mother insists on. She shows an unusually strong craving for candy, though she is allowed but little. She is quite indifferent about her own belongings and lets other children take her toys home without objection. Mrs. Otis says she can't discipline Minerva because she can never tell what the child's feelings are although she seems to be rather contemptuous. She doesn't cry when spanked, merely goes and sits quietly by herself, saying nothing and with her face a blank. Minerva never says "I won't" but she simply fails to do as she has been asked. She is slow to react to friendly advances and is not affectionate. For the past month since in kindergarten, she has fitted into the group satisfactorily and is apparently well liked by the other children, though she is in no way a leader. Minerva appears to be alert and keen, but is too restless to play long with one thing.

Suggested Treatment.—Instead of being responsible to so many people, Minerva should be controlled by only one person, and that probably her grandmother. Her environment should be kept as stable as possible.

Case 64. ARNOLD BJORNSTAD   Five Years and Two Months
Tic. Stutter. Nervous. Grandmother who favors older brother.

Home Situation.—Arnold's family live in a pleasant bungalow on the outskirts of the city. Mr. Bjornstad is a bookkeeper. Except for a slight tic he gives no evidence of nervous instability and is even tempered and intelligent in the handling of his children. Mrs. Bjornstad is a fine woman with considerable poise and great interest in doing what is best for the children. She punishes them by sending them to bed or making them sit still on chairs. Arnold has two brothers, one ten and one a baby.

Developmental History.—Arnold was a placid, happy baby and has been well except for a double mastoid and a tonsillectomy at the age of eleven months. His physical examination at present is negative except for marked thinness, malocclusion of the teeth, and a facial tic. He has an IQ of 105.

History of Adjustments.—Arnold has always had a good appetite, but in spite of this he is considerably underweight. He gives the impression of "worrying himself thin," disturbed perhaps because his grandmother favors his older brother to such a marked degree and continually picks on Arnold. Some months ago he showed a tendency toward enuresis but Mrs. Bjornstad explains this by saying that Arnold was then sleeping with the grandmother and that she required very heavy covers. As soon as he slept in a bed alone the bedwetting disappeared. The only behavior difficulties which Arnold shows at present are a facial tic and a tendency to stutter. His teacher says he is so nervous she thinks he is "on the verge of St. Vitus' dance." His eyes blink almost continually.

Suggested Treatment.—Arnold's parents should speak slowly when addressing him and should absolutely disregard the stuttering. He should have a rest period every afternoon.

Later History.—Two months later Mrs. Bjornstad reports that Arnold's mouth twitches but his eyes no longer blink. He is still stuttering though not to any marked degree. She has been giving him the daily rest period which the physician advised and thinks it has been of great value. Three months later the grandmother paid the family another visit and soon after her arrival Arnold's stuttering increased. He has had another period of bedwetting, but whether this was due to irregularities in his routine during the vacation or due to the presence of the grandmother is not clear. After another month Arnold is in school and enjoying himself, the grandmother has gone home and Mrs. Bjornstad is feeling more at ease about her son.

CASE 65. STANLEY JEFFERSON. FIVE YEARS AND THREE MONTHS
Fears. Night terrors. Feeding problem.

Home Situation.—Stanley and his sixteen year old brother live with their parents in a small, moderately well furnished house. Mr. Jefferson has heart trouble and rheumatism, but in spite of that carries on his work as a painter and is calm and consistent in his treatment of the two boys. His wife, on the contrary, with no actual physical difficulties "never feels well" and exaggerates every minor difficulty in the home. She thinks she is fairly firm with the children but acknowledges that they mind their father better.

Developmental History.—Stanley has always had a poor appetite and is now definitely underweight. He walked and talked at about the usual age and is apparently of average intelligence. He had abscesses in his ears at a year and a half and whooping-cough at age three. Other than that his health has been good.

History of Adjustments.—Stanley refuses to eat any vegetables except the few which his father happens to like. The only other problem which the boy has presented is a fear. Some time ago Stanley's big brother told him of ogres and hobgoblins who lurked in closets and the cellar, and he was much entertained to see the small boy develop a fear of these places. The mother, who has always thought of the child as a baby, has rushed to protect and comfort him. Lately night terrors have developed and a fear of going to sleep unless his mother was in the room.

Suggested Treatment.—The older brother must refrain from his terrorizing tales. Stanley must not become fatigued by playing any boisterous games between school and bed time. He must eat his vegetables before he is given dessert and most important of all, Mr. Jefferson must understand that Stanley's undesirable eating notions are in large part copied from his father.

Later History.—Two months later a social worker called at the house and found that the night terrors were less frequent and that Mr. Jefferson had been most cooperative. When he started setting a good example he discovered, much to his surprise, that vegetables were really good, and he and Stanley are now eating a great variety with pleasure. The mother reported that Stanley still insisted upon her presence in his room when he went to sleep. The child is very suggestible and was evidently impressed when a visitor expressed horror at the thought of so big a boy not going to bed alone. The result was that when Stanley went to bed that night he told his mother she might go away and since then he has never asked her to stay.

CASES 66 AND 67. AVIS BANGS   FIVE YEARS AND THREE MONTHS
                 AMY BANGS   FIVE YEARS AND THREE MONTHS

Twins alike in all reactions, and reported to be identical.

Home Situation.—Mr. Bangs is a sheet metal worker, vigorous, even tempered, and said to be "close mouthed." At home he is loving and friendly with the children. His wife says she is "terribly nervous" and frequently gets to the place where she feels not responsible for her actions. She says she has not had a moment's rest since she was fifteen years old. She appears calm and well-controlled, but tired. She keeps the house in spotless order and although she allows the twins to play in several of the rooms, they are expected to pick up their toys when they have stopped playing. There are also in the home two children of Mr. Bangs by an earlier marriage, a daughter of twenty soon to be married who has never gotten along well with her stepmother, and a brother of fourteen who has fitted into the family well.

Developmental History.—Avis and Amy have always been "as alike as two peas" and have developed at the same rate. Neither was a fretful baby. They always cried simultaneously. Amy walked at sixteen months and Avis only two weeks later. They both began to talk at about a year. Desirable toilet habits were established in both early. Both had whooping cough at the same time. At the present time physical examinations of both children were negative and both received the same IQ, 117. Amy did rather better than Avis on the performance tests.

History of Adjustments.—Both girls bit their nails and sucked their thumbs from babyhood, but now the habits have disappeared entirely in Amy and are occasional only in Avis. On Wednesday of one week Avis was nauseated from no apparent cause, and on the following Saturday Amy showed exactly the same symptoms. Both squinted for a short time before they walked. This Mrs. Bangs thinks was due to sitting facing the sun. Both grind their teeth in their sleep, but Avis somewhat more frequently. Amy never mentions dreams, Avis but seldom. Both have always eaten everything offered and they started feeding themselves at approximately the same time. Both were sent to kindergarten at the age of five. Their teacher says their behavior as well as their appearance is identical. They occasionally fight each other "like cats and dogs" but are ordinarily very devoted. Neither has ever been a behavior problem, except for two times when they ran a short distance away from home. Amy shows somewhat greater interest in reporting the activities at school, and is somewhat more skilled in sewing than Avis. Avis is a bit more popular among the other children, a little more lively and light hearted, and tends to show off a bit more. Both are great talkers.

CASE 68. ELMER NORTH   FIVE YEARS AND FIVE MONTHS

Shocking language. School problem. Impudent. Hyperkinetic.
Annoys other children. No playmates. Over-indulgent grandmother.

Home Situation.—Most of Elmer's relatives on both sides of the family for several generations have been day-laborers and of rather a poor class. The maternal grandfather deserted his family when his children were young. The grandmother, with whom

Elmer has always lived, is said to be "untruthful and unreliable." She has a violent temper and is wholly blind to Elmer's faults. At last accounts, Elmer's father was "bootlegging" liquor which he made himself.   In the first years of his marriage there was continual wrangling between him and his mother-in-law.   Six months before Elmer's birth, Mrs. North obtained a divorce on the ground of "cruel and inhumane treatment."   The father has since attempted to obtain guardianship of the other children but has been judged "unfit to have control of them."   The paternal grandmother seems to be the most stable and reliable relative, and although she quarrels with the others frequently, she nevertheless helps them out when they are ill.   For the past few years Mrs. North has had considerable trouble with stomach ulcers. Two years ago she married a semi-skilled worker in an iron foundry and says she is happier than she has ever been in her life.   Mrs. North gives the impression of a weak, ineffectual woman who has always been dominated by her mother.   She is of the type that allows things to drift along unless some sharp issue arises.   She ignores the faults of her children and it annoys her to be bothered with plans for Elmer as she no longer "allows that subject to disturb her."   Mrs. North has the seven year old brother with her in her new home.   She considers him somewhat backward.   This brother was troubled with enuresis until last year when the grandmother took him home for a week of training, and in that week cured him completely.   The grandmother was so uncooperative that the clinic was unable to learn the method used here.   Elmer's home is a meagrely furnished, squalid shack in a poor neighborhood.   The grandmother does day-work and the boy is left at a day-nursery while she is at work.   His treatment from her at home has been an alternation of pets and cuffs.

Developmental History.—Elmer was not a fretful baby and has always seemed unusually well.   He walked at about a year. Neither mother nor grandmother can remember when he began to talk.   He has had no contagious diseases except measles.   At present the boy appears well-developed and nourished, with no outstanding physical peculiarities.   He has an IQ of 99.

History of Adjustments.—Elmer sleeps quietly and is not easily aroused. He has a good appetite and is not finicky about his food. There has been no stuttering, thumb-sucking or marked enuresis. He has no playmates and has no toys at home except colored newspapers which his grandmother collects for him and which Elmer arranges and re-arranges in all sorts of piles and combinations. He is extremely devoted to his grandmother and calls her "Mama" though he understands perfectly who is his real mother. Only by ruses can the family persuade him to leave the grandmother for even brief stays with his mother.

Four months ago Elmer was sent to kindergarten and he is said to be one of the most difficult children in the group. He wanders about the school-room with no conception of obeying any of the simple kindergarten rules. Lately, however, he has actually accomplished some tasks which he had begun, though his interest has continued to fluctuate more rapidly than that of the other children. He seems to be amenable when personally instructed, but fails to adjust to the group. The teacher thinks that Elmer would improve in his social conduct more rapidly in a smaller group but, of course, the family cannot afford to send him to a private kindergarten. He annoys the other children by biting and pinching them and by destroying their work. They, in turn, find him a nuisance and they fear and avoid him. Elmer is impudent and uses "shocking" language. He is sneaky, refuses to admit anything until he is cornered, is hyper-active and a persistent trouble-maker. He absolutely disregards the rights of others. He delights in being in the center of the stage. He does not cry easily, complain, nor exhibit other neurotic symptoms. His behavior is in all probability due to the indulgence of the grandmother and to the lack of constructive habit-training.

Suggested Treatment.—Elmer should continue in school and should progress to the first grade when his teacher is ready to promote him. He should receive adequate habit-training and training in self-help, and should be praised and encouraged when he does well. His present environment is very unfavorable and Elmer would probably show much more rapid adjustment if he could be placed in better surroundings.

CASE 69. WILSON SCHWARTZ   FIVE YEARS AND SEVEN MONTHS

Fatigue. Negativistic. Annoys other children. Thumbsucking.
Irritable. Many adults in home.

Home Situation.—Wilson and his parents have always lived
with the maternal grandparents and aunt. Various members of
the family show difficult personality traits, and although there is
no open friction in the home there is a constant undercurrent of
irritation. The grandfather is a very moody man who seems
totally incapable of making up his own mind, but who has to be
handled with extreme care if he is to be persuaded to adopt the
suggestions of anyone else. The grandmother is vigorous and
tense and evidently thinks she should dominate not only her
husband's thinking, but that of the entire family group. She
frequently takes over the control of the family and Wilson's
mother then subsides. Mr. Schwartz is now working in a bank
while he studies for the ministry in the hope of becoming a mission-
ary. He is a very particular, finicky man who emphasizes order
and routine. He is fond of Wilson and the two year old sister, but
he is rather exacting and expects prompt obedience. Mr.
Schwartz feels that it would be better to administer prompt physical punishment rather than to use his wife's methods of giving
Wilson time to realize that he is not going to gain his end by his
present actions, but on account of the child's illnesses the father
has not insisted upon a trial of his ideas. Mrs. Schwartz is a
woman of well controlled emotions and sane ideas. She is by
nature very patient, but between her struggles in handling the
grandfather and those in handling her son, she has "reached the
limit of her tact." By the time the day is over she is usually
too exhausted to consider evening recreation, even on the nights
when Mr. Schwartz is not studying.

Developmental History.—Wilson was an extremely fretful
baby and cried almost constantly for two years. He walked at
ten months and talked at fourteen months. He failed to gain
in weight at the expected rate and apparently had severe digestive disorders. Mrs. Schwartz had heard of the marvelous cures
of a glandopath, a man who by placing a peculiarly constructed
metal, rubber and wood arrangement above the various ductless

glands of the body could cure anything from broken bones to chicken-pox. When the treatment was given to Wilson the family noticed improvement both in his digestion and in his disposition which lasted for several days. Wilson has continued to receive treatments nearly every week. The glandopath also recommended the elimination of milk from the boy's diet because it was "congesting the liver." Wilson had a light case of measles at ten months and whooping cough at three years. When examined at the clinic, he was found to be in good general physical condition except for enlarged and diseased tonsils. The physician thought that these might account for Wilson's digestive difficulties. In the intelligence test he received an IQ of 119.

History of Adjustments.—Wilson has a rather poor appetite though he does eat plenty of vegetables. He sucks his thumb when he sleeps and is irritable upon waking. He tires easily. Since the age of two he has shown considerable negativism, particularly toward his mother and grandmother. Temper tantrums were frequent until he was circumcised about three months ago. Mrs. Schwartz has noticed that he is most irritable when he is not in the best physical condition. This irritability shows itself in a nervous cry, a stamping of the feet and a "mulish" desire to fight. He has recently adopted baby talk.

Wilson was sent to kindergarten at the age of five. He is not popular there. When the teacher's back is turned he is apt to poke and pinch the other children. If he is crossed, he sulks; if the others refuse to be dominated by him, he becomes revengeful. He is disagreeable and mean and flies into a rage whenever anything goes wrong. Spanking makes him ugly and rebellious. All of the family feel that the boy is exhibiting traits similar to those of his grandfather and they are naturally much disturbed by this.

Later History.—Five months later Mrs. Schwartz reports that the boy is now a "different being." Since his tonsils were removed two months ago he has been no trouble at all. His digestive disorders have entirely disappeared, his appetite is good, he sleeps better, and with improved physical health has come a corresponding improvement in disposition.

CASES 70 AND 95. GREGORY ANDREWS FIVE YEARS AND SEVEN MONTHS
            LUELLA ANDREWS   SIX YEARS AND TEN MONTHS

Fears.   Temper tantrums.   Cries easily.   Jealous.   Impulsive.
Dependent on mother.   Bedwetting.   Thumb-sucking.   Fatigue.
Daydreams.   Repressed.   Annoys other children.

Home Situation.—The family history of these two children
reveals nothing more than a paternal grandmother with a violent
temper and domineering disposition, and some tendency to nervous tension in the maternal aunts. Mr. Andrews, himself, apparently has inherited his mother's disposition and although fond
of his children, is very exacting and seems to control them through
fear. He is a successful lawyer and provides his family with a
number of luxuries. Mrs. Andrews is highly emotional and
caters to every wish of the children. She is rather hypochondria-
cal, exaggerates her own minor ailments as being due to "nervousness and a naturally weak stomach" and is even more alarmed
if the children show the slightest sign of illness. There are three
other children besides Luella and Gregory, a sister of twelve who
is anaemic and tires easily, a brother of ten who has always been
well, and a sister of two who is "delicate." The home life is in
general harmonious save that the mother feels the father is too
exacting and he feels that she is too indulgent. There is, however, no discussion of discipline before the children.

Developmental History of Luella.—As a small baby Luella
presented practically no problems. She walked and talked at
twelve months. She had a severe case of measles and whooping
cough at two and chicken pox at four. Her tonsils were removed
when she was three. She has been severely frightened several
times and each time her heart has been affected sufficiently to keep
her in bed for several days. Her physical examination at the
clinic was negative. In the intelligence test she received an IQ
of 127 and used a vocabulary as large as that of the average nine
year old child.

History of Luella's Adjustments.—Luella has always been
easily frightened and the family have labored to make her life
smooth and free from terror for fear her heart would be affected.
She has always cried very easily, especially when over-tired. She
is upset at the thought of her mother leaving her for even a few

hours. Temper tantrums are called forth by any slight frustration such as not being able to wear a particular dress or have a particular vegetable at dinner. She sometimes resents any attention her mother may pay to her brothers and sisters, saying "You love them more than you do me." She is very impulsive and shows a few nervous habits like biting her lips when she is absorbed in some task. She is very neat and orderly; is persistent, thoroughly responsible and fair-minded. She acknowledges her own misdeeds and never holds a grudge.

Developmental History of Gregory.—During Gregory's babyhood Mrs. Andrews was obliged to go East on account of her mother's serious illness, and Gregory was cared for almost entirely by nurse-maids and a maiden aunt. They made no attempt to discipline the boy in his mother's absence. He cried a great deal and on Mrs. Andrews' return when he was about a year old he was "frail, weak, and puny." He talked at fifteen months and walked at eighteen months. He had measles at a year, whooping cough at two, chicken-pox at three and had his tonsils removed at four. At present save for some undernourishment, his physical examination is negative. In the intelligence test he received an IQ of 104 and was as well behaved as the average child of seven. He did unusually well on tests involving manual dexterity.

History of Gregory's Adjustments.—Gregory shows a number of infantile traits. Desirable toilet habits were established at the age of a year and a half, but at the age of two he recommenced bedwetting and still does with only occasional omissions. He sucks his thumb, talks baby talk, cries easily, and has a marked craving to be petted and loved. He apparently fatigues easily. Gregory plays well with the baby sister though he cannot get along well with the older children on account of their teasing. In kindergarten he gives the impression of being able to do excellent work if he only cared to, but he daydreams instead. He seems to annoy the other children at school in a spirit of meanness and he is, therefore, not popular. Gregory apparently takes great delight in going counter to the group wishes, makes noises when the teacher starts to tell a story and so on. On the other hand, he responds well if the teacher treats him as an individual rather than as a member of a group. He seems decidedly repressed and shows a definite mother-attachment.

Suggested Treatment.—Mr. and Mrs. Andrews must put less stress on polite manners and more upon self-reliance and proper nourishment. They should ignore Luella's temper tantrums and stop worrying over her supposed tendency to heart trouble. Gregory must not be allowed to be so dependent upon his mother and he should have his afternoon liquids reduced and should be taken up at night to prevent bedwetting. Both children should be provided with constructive toys and a place to play where they are not continually on their best behavior and subject to adult interruptions.

Later History.—Two months later Mrs. Andrews reported that Gregory's bedwetting had practically disappeared. He is now in first grade and reacting well. He considers himself a big boy and has abandoned his baby talk and much of his infantile behavior. He even seems to be making some friends among the other children. Luella has partially given up her temper tantrums and although sometimes unruly, is often charming and lovable.

CASE 71. ALFRED PRIM   FIVE YEARS AND EIGHT MONTHS
       Feeding problem. Temper tantrums. Stuttering. Hyperkinetic.

Home Situation.—Mr. Prim is a mechanic in a large factory and the family live only a few blocks from his work. He stuttered markedly till he was about fifteen but is now a very calm and quiet man, giving no evidence of any nervous disturbance. He is fond of Alfred and the three year old sister but is firm and effective in controlling them. Mrs. Prim is extremely nervous and easily upset. She "goes all to pieces" when she becomes exasperated with Alfred and is then inclined to whip him severely. She is discontented and resents the irksome duties and responsibilities of a home and family. She says that the family life is happy. The social worker at the factory, however, reports that about six months ago there was considerable friction and Mrs. Prim claimed that her husband was unfaithful to her. She went all over the neighborhood seeking evidence against him and contemplated getting a divorce. This seems to have been a temporary storm and in all probability the Prims are not quarreling excessively now.

Developmental History.—Alfred was a fussy, crying baby who at a year showed marked signs of rickets. He walked at twelve months and talked at fourteen. He had whooping cough at two and his tonsils were removed at four. At the present time he is definitely undernourished and his muscles are flabby. He has an IQ of 97.

History of Adjustments.—Alfred has been a difficult feeding problem since infancy. He refuses food no matter how attractively prepared and he particularly dislikes milk and vegetables. "Every meal is a battle." Mrs. Prim claims to have tried punishment, putting to bed, threats, promises of reward, and ignoring all without effect, but probably she has never tried any one method for a sufficiently long period. She admits that he has always lunched between meals. He shows severe temper tantrums when his mother tries to force him to eat but is not in general difficult to handle at other times.

Alfred is a fidgety sleeper. He wet the bed until he was circumcised at the age of four. His speech was clear until he was about two and a half years old. At that time he began to stutter and has since grown markedly worse. Mrs. Prim was at that time punishing Alfred severely when he refused to eat certain foods and she has thought there might be a connection between the two. He stutters at school as badly as at home, and he is very sensitive about his defect. At first his parents tried to make him speak more slowly but this seemed to make him more self-conscious, so they now ignore his speech entirely. The children he plays with, however, often tease him and try to imitate him. The only time that Alfred never stutters is when he sings. Alfred went to kindergarten at the age of five and there he has shown good ability. He is said to be "quick on the up-take." He prefers to play with the older boys and dislikes playing with girls. He is fairly resourceful in entertaining himself but not persistent. He is a good fighter and rather popular with the other children. He is extremely self-conscious, impulsive, restless, fidgety and changeable.

Suggested Treatment.—Alfred needs a calm atmosphere and a freedom from over-stimulation. He also needs relaxation exercises. His diet should be regulated, perhaps by a chart and stars for proper eating. His speech difficulty seems to be the result of general emotional tension.

CASE 72. JASPER SWEET   FIVE YEARS AND NINE MONTHS
    Feeding problem. Fears. Fatigue. Temper tantrums. Cruel.
                        Dislikes school.

Home Situation.—For several generations the Sweets have been regarded as emotional and high-strung. Jasper's father, himself, is hot tempered though he has good control and the mood passes quickly. He holds a responsible position in a large bank and is able to provide his family with many luxuries. Mrs. Sweet is a very intelligent woman who is greatly interested in her children. She is inclined to be over-anxious about her own health as well as that of her children. She objects to leaving them to the care of servants, and as a result spends a great deal of time with them herself. Jasper's ten year old sister is a very studious child who is said to be "nervous." She has an IQ of 113.

Developmental History.—Jasper's health has never been very good. As an infant he was undernourished and rickety. At nine months he had influenza and at three years, whooping cough. He walked at fourteen months and talked at a year and a half. At present he is about average in height and weight but is anaemic and has little resistance. He has enlarged tonsils and considerable adenoid growth, and is a mouth-breather. On the intelligence test he received an IQ of 88.

History of Adjustments.—Jasper has a very capricious appetite and he practically lives on milk. He dislikes all vegetables except carrots and can't eat at all if he sees spinach on the table. Jasper's sister has frightened him by stories of things that might happen in the dark, with the result that he is afraid to be left alone in bed in a dark room. He sleeps quietly, however, when he does go to sleep. The child tires easily and chills easily in winter. He is very clean about himself and his clothes. At the age of five Jasper was sent to kindergarten, but he has never liked it. He says he hates the racket and calls the other children "dumbells." He goes only when he is forced. He learns easily, concentrates well, pays good attention, but never seems really interested. He behaves well and is not mischievous, boisterous, pugnacious or fussy in any way. He is quite decided and not easily led. He is sensitive, but not resentful. He is easily discouraged about his hand-work. He seems to have little imagination, but a large fund of general information. The teacher says he smiles so seldom that it is a treat to them all when he forgets himself and actually enjoys what is going on. He never mingles with the other children and they are, in turn, indifferent to him. He seems to feel above the others in knowledge and experience. Jasper is most interested in the games of the older boys such as football, basketball, etc. When things go wrong he often has temper tantrums in which he screams persistently. At times he seems cruel to his dog and beats it unmercifully. Jasper's own account of kindergarten is that he gets tired with the long walk to school and that when he gets there the other children talk so much they "drive him crazy." He gives the impression of a pale, delicate, slow-moving unenthusiastic child.

Suggested Treatment.—Jasper should be put under the care of a private physician and should have special attention given to his tonsils, adenoids, and anaemia. His fatigue should be met by overfeeding and rest periods. He should be taken out of school until fall and then should enter first grade. If he is still tired by the walk to school, he should be taken in a car.

Later History.—Six months later, Mrs. Sweet reports that Jasper's health has improved during the summer and he seems happier and well. He is enjoying school and making average progress. Mrs. Sweet thinks that some of Jasper's behavior difficulties may be traced back to the fact that his sister has resented the loss of her position as the only child in the family and has consistently tried to "snub" her brother. This aspect of the situation occurred to the parents only after they had spent some months in trying to work out the best possible treatment for the boy's difficulties. After another year, Jasper is reported to have had more rugged health since the removal of his tonsils, and to have a fairly keen interest in school, though he is not progressing in a manner satisfactory to the teacher.

CASE 73. MINNIE WARWICK   FIVE YEARS AND TEN MONTHS
Speech defect.

Home Situation.—Mr. Warwick is a buyer for an importing house and spends at least half his time abroad. He is nervous, high-strung, and easily upset. He seems to have been more or less spoiled by his mother who still babies him and expects to assume control of his home when she visits the family. He stuttered till he was about twenty and still does when he is excited. At home, he is very fond of the children but is firm, tolerates no arguments and never attempts to reason with them. Mrs. Warwick is also pretty tense and speaks very rapidly. She is much interested in planning balanced meals, in keeping the children in excellent physical condition, and in teaching them names of flowers, trees, and birds. The two parents do not agree on discipline. The mother argues with the children, and they rarely obey her promptly. Mr. Warwick becomes very much irritated when the children debate with her. Minnie has an older sister who is nine.

Developmental History.—Minnie was considered a good baby. She walked at eleven months, and began talking at two and a half years. She has always talked baby-talk. She had scarlet fever at six months, and chicken-pox at four years. Her physical examination at present is negative. She received an IQ of 118 and displayed no stuttering during the examination.

History of Adjustments.—Minnie has always been a light eater and rather notional in her likes and dislikes. There has been no enuresis, nail-biting, thumb-sucking, or unusual fear. She began to stutter after she had been in kindergarten two months. She is considered one of the brightest children in the room, speedy in all her reactions, and excellent in hand-work. She is a leader and very popular among the children though not aggressive. She will not tolerate any unkindness on the part of the others. She ignores those who have spoken to her unpleasantly, and if a quarrel occurs, she simply walks off. Minnie is in no way a behavior problem. Her mother thinks her shy and self-conscious, but her teacher calls her very well poised and able to meet different situations well. She is unusually alert and shows excellent concentration. She is very affectionate and exhibits a marked preference for her father.

Case 74. ELEANOR SPENCER   Five Years and Ten Months
Night terrors. Feeding problem.

Home Situation.—Mr. Spencer is the author of a number of widely read serious novels. He is a rather quiet man with a sparkling wit and great cleverness in conversation. Mrs. Spencer is a charming woman who is always eager to help her children and her friends. She is unusually apt in gathering little groups of children in the house and controlling their play so that they are entertained without becoming exhausted. Eleanor has a sister who is not yet two.

Developmental History.—For the first eight months of her life Eleanor was no particular problem, save that she was somewhat underweight, but soon after that she developed a digestive disturbance that required weekly consultations with a pediatrician, and many changes in diet. The difficulty was finally conquered when the child was two and has never returned, but during the year and a half when she was sick, the parents were greatly perturbed and Eleanor seemed to develop neither mentally nor physically as rapidly as might have been expected. Within six months after her digestion had begun to behave properly, the child took great strides in development, is now in excellent physical condition, and large for her age. She had her tonsils removed when she was four, and has had measles during the last year. She has an IQ of 130.

History of Adjustments.—Mrs. Spencer describes Eleanor as of a very nervous temperament, high-strung and emotional. She watches the child constantly to see that she is not becoming overexcited.

Eleanor is extremely devoted to her father and perhaps on this account, refuses to eat the many vegetables which he dislikes.

In addition to these she refuses peas which he happens to eat. Until the last year Mrs. Spencer has insisted that Eleanor eat the vegetables which were given her with the result that every meal ended with Eleanor extremely excited or weeping. Mrs. Spencer felt that she was keeping the child "worked up" all the time, and has for the time being abandoned the attempt to force the child to eat vegetables other than the spinach, asparagus, carrots and onions that she likes.

When Eleanor was about three she began having night-terrors and with a two months intermission last summer has had them practically every night since. They occur regularly between nine and nine-thirty. Many methods have been tried to break them up. Eleanor's diet has been systematically varied until the mother and the physician have been convinced that her food at night had no effect. Mrs. Spencer has tried keeping her very quiet and reading mild stories for the hour before bedtime, taking Eleanor to the toilet ten minutes before the terror was due to arrive, and various methods of wakening her. Although nothing has succeeded in preventing the night terror, the parents have found the best method of soothing her is to go to her bed and talk quietly to her for a few minutes, to let her walk around the house for a short time, or to let her get into bed with her mother temporarily. Mrs. Spencer's own conviction is that the screaming has now become a habit and will persist until the child outgrows it or until some change in the family routine happens to interrupt it. She hopes that a night on the train and a visit to the grandmother this summer will be effective.

CASE 75.   FREDERICK HOLTON   FIVE YEARS AND ELEVEN MONTHS

Nervous. Fatigue. Cries easily. Fears. Thumbsucking. Rebels against discipline. Inhibited. Oversolicitous mother.

Home Situation.—The Holtons live in an upper duplex in a suburban neighborhood. The home is somewhat shabby, but comfortable. Mr. Holton is head of one of the departments in a dry-goods store, and is described as a "typical old maid." He lisps, has a slight tic about one eye, and is rather timid. He has an intelligent interest in the children and cooperates well, though he is neither so keen nor so broad-minded as his wife. In some moods, he tends to tease. Mrs. Holton was a very capable stenographer before her marriage and she still returns at busy periods to help in the office where she worked for several years. She is usually intelligent and interested in training her children according to the soundest methods. She does not believe in preventing a child from following out any of his ideas that are within reason, even though they may be contrary to suggestions which she had made. Some of the relatives think Mrs. Holton humors the children too much. The most effective form of punishment with both Frederick and his seven year old sister has been found to be spanking, but it has not been necessary to punish either of them often.

Developmental History.—As a baby, Frederick was good when at home, but was always fussy away from home or when the home routine was broken for any reason. He walked and talked at about sixteen months. He has had measles, scarlet fever, whooping cough and at the age of three a severe case of acidosis. His physical examination recently was practically negative save for some slight underweight and two carious teeth. In the intelligence test he received an IQ of 106, and did exceptionally well on the performance tests.

History of Adjustments.—Frederick is nervous, tires easily, cries easily, and is easily frightened. He would have temper tantrums if he were encouraged, but when he commences to scream, he is told that if he does not stop he will be given something real to cry over, and he stops immediately. He has never been a feeding problem. He sleeps well but acts dazed and grouchy the first hour after waking. He sucks his thumbs frequently in spite of pepper, various unpleasant substances, tapes, etc. Last year he attended kindergarten, but he did not like it and showed no interest in the kindergarten activities. He likes first grade no better. He is not a leader but he refuses to obey the commands of the other boys. He rebels against discipline, and won't listen to reason though he harbors no resentment after punishment. He often seems inhibited in his actions, loses his nerve when the moment for definite action comes, and frequently is unable to express his feelings. When pressed by necessity, he can rise to an occasion, but he puts it off as long as possible. This appears on such occasions as wanting permission from the teacher to do some little thing which he knows he can do for the asking. Frederick is unusually timid, and in particular is much afraid of fire-engine bells and sirens. When he hears one, he races home immediately, but if he is too far away to get there before the fire-engine passes, he is in a quandary. For he is so afraid of strangers that he dares not go into another person's house, so he jumps up and down on the sidewalk, apparently thus relieving his excitement. He is afraid of ghosts and the bogy-man as the result of stories of his brother and some of the older children. He is also afraid there are mice under his bed when he goes to bed at night. During a recent physical examination, the boy spent most of the time climbing over the arms and back of the chair. This purposeless activity was apparently an expression of embarrassment. Frederick is particularly devoted to his father and loves above everything else to go to walk with him.

Suggested Treatment.—Mrs. Holton is probably over-solicitous, and she should try to curb this tendency in herself. Frederick should have dental attention; he should be sent to school in spite of his dislike; he should be given an over-nourishing diet, and his mother should attempt to develop his social activities.

CASE 76. KARL MUNSON   SIX YEARS AND NO MONTHS
Lisps. Changeable. Stubborn. Hyperkinetic. Imaginative.
Unstable attention.

Home Situation.—Karl lives in a fairly good neighborhood with his father and stepmother. Mr. Munson is an automobile salesman with much vigor and push. He is generally slow to anger but has been known to become provoked and spank Karl soundly. Karl's mother, who died when he was a year old, was not well liked. She was jealous, irritable, irresponsible and exhibited frequent temper tantrums. She was happy at her son's birth but soon lost interest in him. After her death Karl lived with a succession of boarding mothers, some harsh and some overlenient, but none interested enough to give the boy any habit training whatever. When Mr. Munson remarried, Karl returned home. The stepmother is a visionary, emotional woman who is easily upset and for a time last winter "went to pieces." She is genuinely interested in Karl though she misses the stimulation of work in a large office and finds her married life dull and monotonous. She frequently feels humiliated at the child's behavior.

Developmental History.—For the first four months of his life, Karl was a fretful baby, colicky, rickety, and delicate. He walked and talked at about a year and has had no serious diseases. His tonsils and adenoids were removed before the age of three. At present he is fairly well developed though stoop shouldered and poorly nourished. He has an IQ of 106 but he did poorly on performance tests, failed to profit much from experience, followed directions poorly, and fatigued quickly.

History of Adjustments.—Karl exhibits a number of nervous. tendencies. He wet the bed until he was nearly four and he speaks with a decided lisp. He can be a charming child one moment and horrible the next. One day when he was visiting, Karl took the clock apart, threw the friend's apples all over the yard, and so on. He seems to be almost immune to pain, or else to be unusually stubborn. One day he was warned not to play with the mouse trap for fear of catching his fingers. When they were finally caught, Karl insisted that it didn't hurt. Except when spinning his top, the child is seldom still a minute.

At the age of four and a half Karl went to kindergarten and enjoyed it. He is now in first grade and dislikes it. His conduct is poor, he tells long imaginary tales, his attention is flighty and he is unwilling to wait for his turn. He secures attention by such actions as holding one note while the rest of the singing class is two or three measures ahead, thus spoiling the melody of the entire class. Karl does not fight with the other children but they dislike him. In the clinic he objected to being undressed, was over-active, very manic and showed considerable flight of attention.

Suggested Treatment.—Karl's lisp seems to be neurotic, that is, it shows a desire in the child to hold on to babyhood. He should be given a well-rounded diet, correct sleeping habits, plenty of exercise without fatigue, posture work in school, consistent discipline and praise for success.

Later History.—Two months later Karl's stepmother reported marked improvement.

CASE 77. CHESTER MANDIG   SIX YEARS AND ONE MONTH
Feeding problem. Occasional stutter. Worries about school.

Home Situation.—Mr. Mandig left Poland at the age of ten and after trying several types of jobs in this country, has settled down as a janitor. He is a quick tempered, irritable man who expects immediate obedience and becomes furious if his wife allows Chester to "work" her in any way. If Mr. Mandig is feeling indulgent, he will talk to Chester by the hour or make him some elaborate toy, but this friendly mood is likely to be upset at any trifling annoyance. He is not a particularly sociable man and his wife resents his "seclusiveness." She feels that "you can't expect Chester to be well-poised and well-balanced when his father gets mad and flies off the handle all the time," yet she fails to see anything undesirable in the fact that she herself is "too nervous to have a lot of kids running around the house." The result is that Chester, deprived of young companions, is perfectly aware that he is the center of attention and discussion as long as he is awake.

Developmental History.—Chester was not a fussy baby although he had diarrhea throughout his infancy. He walked at seventeen months and talked soon after he was two. His tonsils and adenoids were removed when he was three. He had scarlet fever at five and now has frequent colds. He is well developed and fairly well nourished, but seems to be the high-strung, neurotic type of child. In the intelligence test he received an IQ of 110 and was markedly verbalistic.

History of Adjustments.—Chester is "crazy" over meat, bread, and potatoes, but it is hard to get him to eat other vegetables. When forced to eat against his will, he immediately vomits. He is at present taking cod liver oil and he frequently vomits that though less often than at first. When he vomits his breakfast, his mother gives him the same menu for lunch, feeling that it is willful misbehavior. Sometimes he will vomit again, sometimes refuse to eat it, and sometimes will eat it without complaint. At night Mrs. Mandig is worried if Chester has vomited the two earlier meals and she usually then gives him what he wants to eat. At one time he spent several weeks with an aunt and tried the same tactics with her, but she forced a second meal upon him immediately and this one always stayed down. Chester admitted at the clinic that he could refrain from vomiting if he tried.

Chester is ordinarily happy and jolly but he worries extremely about his school. He is a very conscientious child and gets terribly upset and "panicky" if he is hurried or if he is unable to do things as well as he would like. He cannot sing or skip but he is much interested in reading and at home keeps his parents reading and spelling and teaching him letters. Chester has now been advanced to the first grade in the hope that with a calmer atmosphere his school difficulties will disappear. He does get on somewhat better, but occasionally becomes so excited when he begins a sentence that he stutters. A year ago he was over-dependent upon his mother but this situation was relieved by the visit to the aunt mentioned above.

Suggested Treatment.—Mr. and Mrs. Mandig should agree on a method of discipline and there should be no interference with each other's orders. Other children should be encouraged to come to the house to play with Chester. Mrs. Mandig should cultivate more poise and should speak more slowly. Chester should hear no remarks about his nervous vomiting and stuttering and he should accomplish nothing by either of these habits.

Later History.—After seven months Mrs. Mandig reports that Chester has not vomited since he was at the clinic, and that his behavior has changed completely since the arrival of a baby sister. Instead of being a baby who requires attention, he is now a "big brother." He still tends to stutter.

CASE 78. EVERETT FREDERICKSON   SIX YEARS AND ONE MONTH
Fidgety in school. Nervous. Excitable. School problem.

Home Situation.—Mr. Frederickson is a repair man for a telephone company, and a good steady worker. He spends considerable time with his family. He is even-tempered, gentle, and quiet in all his dealings with his children. If one of the children misbehaves, the father explains in simple terms why the action was wrong, and punishes him gently; but if the offense is repeated, the punishment is next time more severe. His wife considers him an excellent disciplinarian. She herself seems to have a keen grasp of the situation and shows much good common sense, although she has great difficulty in expressing herself and apparently has a deep feeling of social inferiority. She does not mix with people easily and seldom goes out. She is nervous and "goes to pieces" under strain and difficult situations. Mrs. Frederickson believes, however, that she never shows her nervous excitability in handling the children, and never lets her voice betray her feelings. A sister, age eleven, is a bright, vigorous girl who does well in school and is very proud of the twins Everett and Sydney. Sydney is a quiet, bashful type, very much of a follower. He is much attached to his twin brother, and feels badly about Everett's school failure. The teacher reports that Sydney is nervous, but does average work, and seems able to apply himself better than Everett. All the members of the family are very fond of each other, and depend on each other for recreation. If one of the twins is punished, the other feels badly and soon has his arms around him or is shedding tears with him.

Developmental History.—Everett was a crying, fretful baby, but not colicky. He walked and talked soon after he was a year old. At the age of one month he had a mild case of whooping cough, and since then has had scarlet fever, pneumonia, and measles twice, (once followed by abscesses in the ear). When three years old he was hit by a truck and badly frightened, though only slightly injured. For some six months after this experience he was very nervous and stuttered markedly. His physical examination at the present time is negative except for moderately infected tonsils. In the intelligence test he received an IQ of 97 while his twin brother received one of 126.

History of Adjustments.—Both the twins are somewhat afraid of the dark, but providing each of them with a flash light to keep under his pillow, seems to have solved that difficulty. Sydney has shown no problem at all and gets along well in school. He gives up to Everett easily. Everett is somewhat finicky about his food, but his fancies are not catered to. There has been no history of nailbiting, thumbsucking, or bedwetting. The school reports that he is fidgety and restless, but Mrs. Frederickson says he is not that way at home. At the age of four Everett began to take mail out of nearby mailboxes, and papers from paperstands. His purpose was apparently merely to add to a collection of papers which he was hoarding at home. At four and a half the twins were sent to kindergarten, and were not regarded as problems there although they were more active and got into more mischief than the average child. At five and a half they entered first grade, but six weeks later Everett was dismissed. The teacher's explanation was that he was extremely nervous and acted much like a child with St. Vitus' dance. An instance of his behavior was his great excitement at a slight hammering in the steam pipes which went unnoticed by the others. Besides this, he did such things as crawl around under the desks, stick pins into the other children, and pinch their legs. There were even more serious difficulties, for several times he took money and candy from the other desks. These were apparently not intended for the boy's own use but were to be given to others. The teacher insists that she did not consider the petty thieving sufficiently important to expel the child, but she did think his general behavior a very bad influence in the class-room. Mrs. Frederickson at this time kept Everett home for two weeks. He was pleased when allowed to return once more to school, but after a trial of three days, he acted as erratically as ever. This time the Fredericksons removed him and sent him to a parochial school. Everett now felt disgraced, cried for a whole day, and was very sensitive to the inquiries of neighbors. In the new school his expression is often worried, unhappy, and scowling. He proves once more to be nervous, fidgety, and tense, he is cons' intly out of his seat or in the aisle and at times stutters. When the teacher took hold of his arm to help him with writing, he jerked away and became rigid. His school work is about average, and he gets on fairly well with the other children. He is always the aggressor and the leader, though not intractable. He never complains or whines at home when he has been "licked" in a fight. If Everett happens to like a person he will go to great effort to please him; but if he dislikes anyone, he delights in annoying behavior.

Suggested Treatment.—Since there is a definite difference in the mental ability of the two twins, they should not be allowed to attend the same school, and Mrs. and Mr. Frederickson must be careful not to compare Everett unfavorably with Sidney. Everett should be encouraged to collect something more worth while than papers. If possible he should be made a monitor or be given some responsibility at school.

CASE 79. NETTIE FRIZZELL   SIX YEARS AND TWO MONTHS
Excitable. Distractible. Fatigue.

Home Situation.—When Nettie was two years old she was adopted by a fairly well-to-do family. Until that time she had lived in a variety of boarding homes, none particularly good, and none particularly bad. She calls her adoptive parents "Mother" and "Father" and we shall refer to them in that way. Mr. Frizzell has a responsible position in a series of chain stores and he frequently is away from home for six weeks at a time. He is an even-tempered man, very fond of his own child, a boy of eight, and of Nettie. He tends to spoil the children when he is at home, but they both mind him well. Mrs. Frizzell is a bright, intelligent woman with considerable business ability. She helps her husband with records and reports.

Developmental History.—When Nettie became a member of the Frizzell family she was badly malnourished. She had been able to sit up alone for only a few months and did not talk at all. Before she reached the age of two and a half she had had rickets, mumps, pneumonia, whooping-cough, and measles. At present she is somewhat undersized and frail looking. Her feet are not well developed, her ankles and legs have a rather twisted appearance, and her motor control is poor. She has an unpleasant odor in spite of frequent baths. On the intelligence test she received an IQ of 97.

History of Adjustments.—Nettie displays few adjustment difficulties. She sleeps and eats well, has no night terrors, no fears, no temper tantrums, and no nervous habits. She reacts well to punishment and harbors no resentment. She is social, generous, demonstrative and affectionate.

Six months ago Nettie was sent to kindergarten where she learns quickly but her hand and rhythm work are not particularly good. The teacher has recommended promotion and Mrs. Frizzell wishes advice as to placing her in first grade. She is somewhat disturbed because Nettie has seemed so susceptible to fatigue while in kindergarten. She has been excitable, played hard, and at times cried hard. When she lies down to rest she "is so quiet and exhausted she looks as if she were dead." She would be a leader among the children if it were not for the fact that it seems impossible for her to keep her attention on any one thing for any length of time.

Suggested Treatment.—Nettie should have a well regulated regimen of diet, exercise and rest. She should complete this year in kindergarten because she needs work in rhythm and motor control. Her parents should encourage games which tend to develop motor control.

Later History.—A year later Nettie is found to be a pound over-weight. Her unpleasant odor and to some extent her "nervousness" have disappeared since she was treated for worms last summer. She is still fidgety in school and enters into all activities with over-much zest and intensity, but does not fatigue as quickly as formerly. She has lost some of her extreme sensitiveness, is now in grade 1-A, is doing excellent work and is very happy in school. Her IQ at the present time is 103.

CASE 80. BOBBY SHAW   SIX YEARS AND TWO MONTHS

Nervous. Irritable. Swears. Disobedient. Shy. Cries easily.
Nervous habits. Nervous father.

Home Situation.—Bobby's father is an insurance agent. He is impatient and becomes irritated when Bobby and the baby sister do not obey promptly. When he comes home at night he assumes charge of the children and usually feeds them and puts them to bed. He thinks his wife is too "easy." Mrs. Shaw is a rather frail woman who purposely indulges the children because she remembers her own unhappy childhood. She acknowledges that she is easily annoyed by Bobby's behavior but claims that she is more patient than his father. Threats, entreaties, spanking, deprivations, and ignoring the child's conduct have all been tried as discipline. The last two have proved most effective.

Developmental History.—Bobby had no difficulties in his first year and he walked and talked at twelve months. At a year and a half he had diphtheria immediately followed by whooping cough and pneumonia. His tonsils and adenoids were removed soon after he was two and he had chicken-pox and scarlet fever at five. He is now fairly well developed and nourished. On the intelligence test he received an IQ of 116.

History of Adjustments.—Mrs. Shaw describes Bobby as a "nervous, irritable, but somewhat lovable child." He sleeps soundly though he complains that his legs ache at night. Until the last few months he had to be forced to eat vegetables. Now he eats everything. He is impulsive and constantly on the go. He swears, is defiant when punished and then continues to disobey.

At school in the first grade he is said to be restless, shy, and not a leader. He has a tendency to brag but he does not blame others for his misdeeds. The teacher considers him good in school work and no trouble. He likes to boss the younger children and the neighbors call him a fighter. Bobby frequently has crying spells when compelled to dress himself in the morning instead of playing, when required to put on his old clothes before going out to play, and when asked to do any little chore around the house. Last year for a time, he twitched his face in a stereotyped manner. He now sniffs. This appears most often when he is excited or self-conscious and Mrs. Shaw thinks it is done to gain attention.

Suggested Treatment.—Bobby's parents must insist on his dressing himself promptly without argument. Since Mr. Shaw is very nervous and irritable when he gets home at night, it might help the general situation if the children were fed by their mother before the father gets home. Then they could play quietly while he has a chance to relax and recover his poise before coming into contact with them.

Later History.—Three months later, Mrs. Shaw reported that Bobby had stopped crying since she had been more firm with him. He is still sniffing considerably, but his mother has observed that it is less frequent when ignored by everyone.

CASE 81. JEANETTE YOUNG   SIX YEARS AND THREE MONTHS

Nailbiting. Finger-sucking. Restless sleep. Distractible. Imaginative.

Home Situation.—Jeanette's father is an alert and successful dentist. In his treatment of Jeanette and her two year old sister he is calm and even tempered and they obey him promptly. Mrs. Young is a very frivolous woman who has had one "nervous breakdown" and gives the impression of being "spoiled." She is deeply interested in the children and very conscientious but she worries about Jeanette's progress in school, is easily upset by the children's conduct and nags them.

Developmental History.—Jeanette was a good and a healthy baby. She walked at twelve months and spoke clearly at sixteen months. Her tonsils and adenoids were removed when she was three and a half. Except for mumps at age four, she has had none of the common children's diseases. At the present time her physical examination is negative. She has an IQ of 120 with a reading ability somewhat less than the average for her age.

History of Adjustments.—As a small child Jeanette had no playmates. Her mother went to some social gathering almost every afternoon and left the child in the care of a maid who was either too lazy or too thoughtless to provide small companions. Jeanette has always been surrounded with a mass of poorly selected toys, and then expected to amuse herself. When her mother came home the child was treated as a plaything herself, dressed up and shown off. She was regularly drilled in nursery rhymes and stories by an aunt. Jeanette has always been a rather eccentric eater, but in this Mrs. Young has been very firm and has expected her to eat what was set before her. A year ago Jeanette began to bite her nails; nine months later she stopped, but she has now begun again. She sucks the first two fingers of one hand in spite of many devices.

She is a restless sleeper and sometimes cries out for two or three nights in succession. She will then sleep quietly for a few nights. Jeanette is very amenable to discipline and very affectionate. She is evidently quite suggestible and has taken over many of the manners and habits of the adults around her. Mrs. Young considers her "nervous." Jeanette spent two months in a private and a year in a public kindergarten. She is now in grade 1-B. In school she is said to be "very attractive and lovable though erratic and very distractible." She has an unusually lively imagination. When a story is told by the teacher or by one of the other children, Jeanette always volunteers another story a bit more thrilling and insists that it is true. She will acknowledge it as make-believe only after a long attack. Jeanette occasionally yells out in school for no apparent reason.

Suggested Treatment.—Jeanette should be provided with constructive toys and should no longer be shown off. She should have specific help at school in reading. Mrs. Young must not try to help her with her reading at home for there would probably be a confusion in the two methods. The difference between reality and phantasy should be pointed out to the child in order to avoid the possibility of her becoming too wrapped up in phantasy.

CASE 82. PEARL SIMS   SIX YEARS AND THREE MONTHS
Fears.   Temper tantrums.   Handles genitals.   Restless.   Boisterous.
     Obstinate.   Hyperkinetic.   Too high standards.   Nervous mother.

Home Situation.—Pearl comes from nervous stock on both sides of the family. Her paternal grandmother and aunt have had nervous breakdowns. Her maternal grandfather is a high-strung, explosive type of man. Mr. Sims is an alert advertising man who is in general even-tempered, but is easily irritated, and demands absolute obedience. Mrs. Sims is an extremely nervous, sensitive woman who is easily upset and exhausted. She says frankly that she is unable to cope with the home situation. She is sure she is absolutely unfit to be a mother and thinks the children would be better off if she were dead. The children resent her approaches and defy her with "I won't" and "I don't have to." They stall and loiter at every demand she makes. Then she becomes upset, cries and harangues about their misbehavior long after the incident has passed. The children are a continual disappointment to her. It is probable that since Pearl is over-sized and boisterous, she frequently embarrasses her refined and rather dignified mother, and reminds her of the unstable aunt. The brother, aged eight and the sister aged four also are hard to manage. Mr. Sims is very much annoyed when he comes home and finds the house in a state of turmoil and the mother upset. On these occasions he punishes the children severely.

Developmental History.—Pearl was regarded as a good, healthy baby though there was some tendency toward rickets. She talked at one year and walked at seventeen months. Since she was two she has had measles, chicken pox, and scarlet fever. Her tonsils and adenoids were removed at four and glasses for strabismus were provided at that age. She is about ten pounds overweight and has the physique of an eight year old child. In the intelligence test she received an IQ of 83. Here she was very curious and uncontrolled, lacking in resourcefulness, and very distractible.

History of Adjustments.—Up to the age of four, Pearl is said to have been a "terrific" feeding problem but she is now eating well. Until she entered kindergarten her temper tantrums were so violent that the only way her mother could restore her was to throw cold water in her face. She is a very light sleeper and afraid of thunder and wind storms although no one else in the family is similarly affected. Until recently Mrs. Sims has been greatly worried at the child's tendency to handle her genital organs. All sorts of treatments have been tried; ignoring, lying down on the bed with her till she is asleep, giving frequent baths, etc. Now that her mother allows her to suck her thumb when she goes to bed, the other habit has practically disappeared. Pearl attended a nursery school for four months and at age of five went to kindergarten. In the kindergarten Pearl was very restless, boisterous, "bossy," and consequently unpopular with the other children. She was extremely restless, and dashed from one thing to another. She was also obstinate and often refused to join the group activity. At times, however, the child was very friendly and seemed to have a "sweet" personality. She is not persistent in any play. Until the last few months she has been unable to sit still long enough to listen to even the most entertaining story. Pearl liked Sunday School very much but was so impulsive and aggressive there that the family were asked to remove her. This year Mrs. Sims insisted on her promotion to the first grade because she was so over-sized, although the kindergarten teacher considered her undeveloped in power of concentration and poor in handwork.

Suggested Treatment.—Mrs. Sims must realize Pearl's mental limitations and simplify her life at school and at home as much as possible. She must not try to form more than one habit at a time, must show affection for the child and praise her when she does well. If they could afford to send Pearl to a good boarding school, that might relieve the situation considerably.

CASE 83. JERRY ZUREK   SIX YEARS AND FOUR MONTHS
School problem. Unintelligent parents.

Home Situation.—Jerry's paternal grandmother has made several attempts to establish the Zurek family on a sound basis by equipping an apartment for them and so on, but all these attempts have been unsuccessful. Mr. Zurek is a "chronic deserter" and is now in the reformatory for non-support of his family. Although he was always good-natured at home and extremely kind to Jerry, he was hot-tempered and had great difficulty in getting along with the other workers in any of the factories where he has been employed. He quarrels violently as well as frequently, is a gambler and "no good." Mrs. Zurek is more cooperative but has difficulty in expressing herself in English. She works as a laundress. Mrs. Zurek is very changeable, not dependable, inclined to alcoholism, and apt to do inexplicable things, such as wiring her husband's relatives that one of her children was very ill and requesting money, when the child wasn't sick and she had no particular need for money. She is vacillating and tells many stories which don't hang together. She is an inadequate homemaker, failing to furnish a suitable diet for the children, and appearing absolutely indifferent about their hours and discipline. Jerry's sixteen year old half-brother is living with his grandmother, but the thirteen year old brother, and the three year old sister (who is rated as "superior") are living with Jerry and their mother in a light-housekeeping arrangement of one room and an alcove. Both Mr. and Mrs. Zurek have been given intelligence tests and their IQ's are, respectively, 66 and 74. Even in consideration of Mrs. Zurek's difficulty with English, there seems little chance that she would rate as "average" in intelligence.

Developmental History.—Mrs. Zurek cannot remember much of Jerry's development, save that at the age of three she took him to a clinic and the doctor said he had rickets. At present he is somewhat under-nourished, and has many dental caries. In the intelligence test he received an IQ of 90, repeated questions, and showed some instability, delayed responses, and poor habits of work.

History of Adjustments.—Between the mother's language difficulty and her general indifference to the children, it was impossible to secure from her more information beyond the facts that Jerry started first grade at the age of six and that the teacher says he acts more babyish than the others and doesn't apply himself. Mrs. Zurek herself does not consider him a behavior problem. In the clinic he was friendly and talkative. He fidgeted and twisted about a great deal, seemed fairly happy and not repressed.

Suggested Treatment.—Mrs. Zurek should provide a better regulated diet for all the children. Jerry's teeth should receive immediate attention. He should continue in first grade, and if possible should have motor and habit training.

CASE 84. RICHARD MORRIS   SIX YEARS AND FOUR MONTHS
Helplessness. Poor motor control. Over-sheltered.

Home Situation.—Within the last ten years the Morris family have risen from "comfortable" finances to considerable wealth. This has been accomplished partly thru inheritances and partly thru the intelligence and business acumen of Mr. Morris. Mrs. Morris is a well educated, very attractive woman, who is sometimes referred to as a "social climber." Richard's two sisters, aged twenty-one and eighteen, were born before the family had acquired any great amount of wealth and they are both attractive and capable young women, well able to look out for themselves.

Developmental History.—Richard is said to have been a well baby and is thought to have walked and talked at about the usual time, though his mother was then so taken up with her social engagements that she left Richard's care entirely to a highly recommended nurse maid. He has had no serious diseases and at the present time is a well developed, fairly well nourished boy. He is very awkward, quite fidgety at times and shows such poor motor control as to suggest chorea. His physical examination, however, was negative save that his muscles were rather flabby and he had relatively little strength. He graded well on intelligence tests with an IQ of 125.

History of Adjustments.—Richard's older sister, Esther, brought him to the clinic in some alarm, fearing that he was feebleminded. The story she told was as follows: Richard's nursemaid had been given a holiday and Esther, who was home from college on a vacation, had taken Richard to see some old friends. When she had tried to dress her brother for the trip, she found he was utterly helpless, couldn't button up his clothes, or lace his shoes or in any way assist in dressing. Articles which he picked up were held clumsily or dropped. During their half-hour on the train the child kept up a sort of quiet fidgeting, but failed, according to Esther, to display the curiosity and interest of a normal child. In order to reach the friend's house, it was necessary to cross a street. Esther started ahead but before she reached the other side she was stopped by a wail from Richard. There he stood in the middle of a big mud puddle crying in a helpless manner. His sister was provoked. Her scolding brought forth the timid explanation "I didn't know it was wet." Esther was then fully disturbed about Richard's mental condition and brought him to the clinic for advice.

Suggested Treatment.—The child must no longer be treated as a baby. The nurse must insist that he rely on himself, and must allow him to learn from experience even if that experience entail dirt, fatigue, and minor bumps. A change of nurse maids would probably be beneficial. He should have specific practice in dressing, and should be provided with toys or play equipment that involve much muscular activity.

CASE 85. OWEN SWANSON   SIX YEARS AND FIVE MONTHS
    Hyperkinetic. Fatigue. Excitable. Irritable. Nervous.

Home Situation.—Mr. Swanson is the minister in a fairly large Congregational church. He is an easy-going man with high ideals and a great deal of friendly interest in his four children. Mrs. Swanson is an attractive, rather high-strung woman who endeavors to bring her children up wisely. The ten-year-old sister shows some nervous habits such as sucking her thumb if over-tired. There are two children younger than Owen, a brother of five with whom he plays happily and a baby sister. The punishments used most often are scolding, putting to bed, and spanking, and the parents are extremely careful never to interfere with each other's discipline. Owen objects to his father's reproofs more than to those of his mother.

Developmental History.—Owen was a very fussy baby. He cried frequently, slept little, and at three months gave definite signs of rickets. He walked at thirteen months and talked at sixteen months. He had measles at four years, and chicken pox a few months later. At present he is a tall, slight boy somewhat underweight. His tonsils are large and protruding. On the intelligence test he received an IQ of 120.

History of Adjustments.—Owen's appetite is fairly good, but he dislikes vegetables. He is hyperkinetic and has been "busy every minute since he was born." For the last year and a half Owen has not looked well, he has tired easily, especially if excited from playing with many other children. Some nights he has been so tired that he has dropped asleep at the supper table. He ordinarily has great difficulty in getting to sleep, and some time ago the family physician prescribed bromides, and also recommended only a half day at school and a rest period in the afternoon. He has no nervous habits like thumb-sucking or nail-biting, but for a time last fall his body seemed to twitch at night. He resents criticism and punishment, and often reacts by sulking or by assuming a bravado air. If he once forms a habit, he has great difficulty in breaking it. At the age of five Owen was sent to a public school kindergarten and some months later promoted to the first grade. Here he failed to make a good adjustment. His hand work was excellent, but his reading much below the average. If corrected or if urged to work faster, Owen resorted to crying or sulking and sometimes even became so excited that he turned white. He did better when the work was individual and when he was praised, but he seemed exhausted by the contact and competition with the large group of children. When this situation became clear, Owen was placed in a private school with only fifteen children in his grade. His new teacher is much interested in him, allows him to stay at home afternoons and is careful to change his task when she sees that he is becoming discouraged or excited. When he shows a tendency to cry, she gives him a task in which he can excell and be praised.

Suggested Treatment.—Since physical inferiority may account for Owen's fatiguability and irritability, he should be placed under a well-regulated routine of exercise, rest, and diet. His nose and throat should be examined by a specialist to determine the advisability of having tonsils and adenoids removed. He should have help in reading easy stories for pleasure until good reading habits are established. He should be encouraged in forming habits of independence and self-help.

Later History.—Six months later Mrs. Swanson reported that the family had been out of the city for several months on account of the serious illness of the grandmother, and that while at the grandmother's home instead of going to school Owen had been tutoring in reading with a remarkably good teacher. His reading has improved to such an extent that he now is up to the level of the reading of the other children and most of his extreme excitability and tenseness has disappeared.

CASE 86. GERTRUDE FRYE   SIX YEARS AND FIVE MONTHS

Feeding problem. Temper tantrums. Petty stealing. Hard to manage.
Expelled from school because of threat to kill the teacher.
Psychopathic father.

Home Situation.—The Fryes live in a shabby four room house which is clean but in poor repair. Gertrude's father has been diagnosed as a case of "constitutional psychopathic inferiority" and is probably also retarded mentally. He has never stuck to any one job long enough to earn an adequate living for his family, and for the last six years they have received frequent financial assistance from various charities. Some time ago Mr. Frye became incensed at one organization and threatened to kill any social worker who came near his house. At another time he announced his intention of going to Washington to "shoot up the whole government." He has advised the school authorities to whip Gertrude severely. In spite of this record he impresses the casual visitor as rather an amiable person. Mrs. Frye seems to be perfectly satisfied with her husband and bows to his mandates. Her facial expression is one of irritability and her voice is loud and harsh. In spite of the fact that her father beats her more frequently than her mother does, Gertrude is more fond of him. The other children in the family are a seven year old sister who is "docile" and has an IQ of 85, a brother of four said to be spoiled, and a sister of two. The parents openly make comparisons between the children and these comparisons are always to the disadvantage of Gertrude. As the child says herself "My mother would laugh if you told her I could do anything right. She says my sister knows more than I ever will."

Developmental History.—Gertrude was not a fussy baby but sometimes objected to being handled. She walked at eighteen months and talked at about two years. At one year she was said to have rickets and chronic bronchitis. At two she had badly swollen glands. At present she shows fair development and nutrition, moderately enlarged tonsils and several carious teeth. She has an IQ of 86.

History of Adjustments.—Gertrude is a finicky eater, likes only a few vegetables and gags when other foods are forced upon her. She stuttered for a few months last year, but Mrs. Frye thinks this was the result of teasing on the part of her playmates. She displays temper tantrums and her mother has to "hit her hard to get her out of them." She shows no affection toward anyone except her father and the baby.

At the age of five Gertrude was sent to kindergarten and a year later was promoted to first grade. After two months in this room she was expelled as "incorrigible, subnormal, very stubborn, dishonest (on the ground that she took a nickel from a box of money belonging to the class and several apples from the lunches of other children) and vicious (on the ground that she threatened to have her father kill the teacher.)" The teacher seems for some reason to have resented Gertrude's behavior as somehow a personal insult to herself. Other teachers in the building agree that Gertrude is undoubtedly a difficult child to manage, but they feel that in time a sympathetic teacher could understand her and gain her confidence. When interviewed at the clinic, Gertrude smiled mischievously when she acknowledged her threat against the teacher, and implied that everybody talks that way.

Suggested Treatment.—It seemed probable that Gertrude was too immature for kindergarten when she was sent, and so is not yet ready for the work of first grade. It was suggested that she be returned to kindergarten for the rest of this year, under a new teacher if possible and next year make a fresh attempt at first grade with another new teacher. The Frye home seems a poor environment for any child; the parents have neither sufficient intelligence nor sufficient interest to modify their treatment of the children, but there is little chance of placing the children in a more favorable environment.

CASE 87.   PETER CELUSNAK   SIX YEARS AND FIVE MONTHS

Nervous. Fidgety. Twitches. School problem. Feeling of inferiority. Actual physical and mental inferiority.

Home Situation.—Peter's father came to this country from the Balkans when he was eighteen and has been fairly successful. The family live in an upper duplex that is poorly furnished but neat and quite attractive. They own a Ford. Mr. Celusnak is a quiet man who is rather stern with the children. Peter is somewhat afraid of him and is therefore more clumsy in his father's presence. Mrs. Celusnak occasionally tells her husband to let the child alone but in general the parents uphold each other's discipline. Mrs. Celusnak looks nervous and worried. She is always jumping up after some one of the children. An older sister is a mild mental defective but the younger brother and sister have shown no peculiarities.

Developmental History.—Peter was somewhat slow in walking and did not talk until he was two years old. His mother attributes this slowness to the fact that he was then living with his grandmother who is very quiet and seldom speaks. He has, however, always seemed slower than other children of his age. He has had chicken pox, measles and mumps and has frequent headaches. His eyesight is poor and he wears glasses. At the present time he is definitely small for his age and considerably undernourished. He has an IQ of 85.

History of Adjustments.—Peter did not stand out as a definite problem until he entered the first grade just before he was six years old. Here the teacher commented that he acted like a four year old. He was nervous and fidgety, not able to keep still or to hold things without dropping them. He also developed a twitch in one eye. At home Peter had no difficulties. He was shy, obedient, truthful and affectionate. When scolded he is sometimes so frightened he stands still and cannot answer. He is rather cowardly and plays only with younger children. He appears to be inadequate in meeting any situation at all strange.

Suggested Treatment.—Peter should be removed from school for several months. He needs to be built up physically by correct diet, outdoor play and rest. Mrs. Celusnak must not try to shield him too much. Peter should not be pushed.

Later History.—After staying out of school for six months, Peter was tried again in first grade. This time there have been no difficulties. It was apparently a case of a feeling of inferiority based upon actual physical and mental inferiority. After another six months Peter seems more mature, has gained in height and weight, is much more at ease and shows greater spontaneity. He now displays no definite symptoms of inferiority. He is doing fairly well in school.

CASE 88. JESSICA COBB   SIX YEARS AND FIVE MONTHS
   (see case 39)

CASE 89. ALBERTA MARTIN   SIX YEARS AND FIVE MONTHS
   Stubborn. Disobedient. Runs away. Father probably psychopathic.

Home Situation.—Mr. Martin is a nervous, quick tempered
man who has spent several periods in reform schools and work
houses. He is said to be able to "lie as fast as he can talk," to be
"rude and impossible" and to have beaten his first wife (Alberta's
mother). He is, however, well thought of by the plumber who
employs him. Alberta's mother seems to have been a weak sort
of woman who never complained of the harsh treatment she received from her husband. She died when Alberta was two years
old. Mr. Martin's present wife is shiftless and easy-going and
thinks that whatever her husband does is all right. She never
interferes with his severe handling of the children. There is a
nine year old brother who is said by the father to be well behaved
and bright and an eight year old brother who once was a problem
but has had his "spirit broken by discipline." Neighbors have
reported Mr. Martin to the police on account of his abuse of the
children and he was once sent to the workhouse. There is also
a baby step-sister who so far has escaped mistreatment, although
her mother seems as neglectful of and as uninterested in her as
in the other children. The Martins live in a shabby flat over a
grocery store in a neighborhood where there is a great deal of
heavy traffic.

Developmental History.—Alberta was not a particularly fretful baby as far as anyone can remember. She walked at ten
months and talked at sixteen months. She has had chicken pox,
measles and whooping cough, has a poor appetite and is thin and
underweight. She has an unusually small head, and has a habit
of throwing it from side to side. Alberta has an IQ of 99.
Throughout the examination she seemed worried and anxious
and her mind seemed occupied with her own difficulties.

History of Adjustments.—When Alberta's mother died, she
went to live with her maternal grandmother. Here she was apparently happy and presented no problem. However, when Mr.
Martin remarried he insisted upon having the child returned to

him. He has shown considerable jealousy of this grandmother and it is for this reason, probably, that Alberta is allowed to visit her so seldom. The visits, few as they are, seem to constitute Alberta's sole pleasure.

Her father punishes Alberta for such offenses as refusing to try to tie her shoes and for not being neat about her clothes or person. He claims she is stubborn and disobedient; a maternal aunt replies that these characteristics have developed as a result of the father's abuse, and cites such favorable characteristics as the good care she takes of the baby, her love of pretty things, and her quickness in observing and learning to do anything done by hand. Six months ago the child was sent to kindergarten. She did not adjust well and was later promoted to first grade. Here she does well in hand work but in nothing else.

The first time Alberta ran away from home a stranger found her, took her to a restaurant, gave her a good meal and candy and then took her home. On another occasion she was crying when a woman asked her name. She replied that she was "Alberta Wood, and her father had died and was to be buried that day and that her mother worked nights." The police who were then notified, told the woman that this often happened with Alberta and that her parents made no effort to find the child. In the clinic Alberta was very shy. The father gave the impression of a psychopathic personality. He feels that people are persecuting him and trying to alienate the affections of his children.

Suggested Treatment.—Alberta has received pleasurable sensations when she has run away from home. This has probably made her realize more than ever the dire situation at home, and has made her the more eager to escape. The child should be placed outside the home permanently, should attend one of the free summer camps if possible, and should have supervised recreation and some pretty clothes.

CASE 90. KENNETH HUNT   SIX YEARS AND FIVE MONTHS
                  Speech defect. Obstinate.

Home Situation.—Kenneth lives with his parents, a nine year old brother and a four year old sister in a neighborhood of hard-working, thrifty people. The home life is said to be peaceful and happy in spite of the fact that there seems to be some nervous instability in the parents. Mr. Hunt is restless and quick tempered though he is well liked and a good mixer. He drank heavily at the time Kenneth was born but he has practically stopped now and the firm for whom he is bookkeeper regard him as an excellent and steady worker. Mrs. Hunt is inclined to be nervous and shy. She is very moody and is strangely affected by the weather, depressed by cloudy weather and exhilarated by sunshine.

Developmental History.—After three months of colic Kenneth was such a good baby that his mother "scarcely knew she had him." For a year he did nothing but eat, sleep, and grow. He walked at eighteen months but did not talk until he was four years old. He was so inactive his wants were few and most of these few were anticipated by his mother. This, added to the fact that he played alone most of the time, made it unnecessary for him to talk. He is now over-sized, clumsy and slow moving. The only serious disease he has had was measles at the age of three. On the intelligence test he received an IQ of 83 and the examiner reports that this low rating was not due to inability to express himself.

History of Adjustments.—Kenneth has a good appetite. He sleeps well and wets the bed only when he has a cold. Mrs. Hunt is disturbed chiefly over the fact that Kenneth did not talk at all before he was four and speaks very indistinctly now. She acknowledges, however, that since he has been attending school (he is now in grade 1-B) his speech has improved noticeably. His teacher says that he never shows by his facial expression whether a remark has penetrated or not. Kenneth resents authority, objects to being hurried, is often obstinate, and dislikes getting dressed and undressed, but he is liked by other children. He lies occasionally to shield himself. When asked what he liked to do best, he answered "Sleep."

Suggested Treatment.—Kenneth should have careful speech training.

Later History.—Five months later his teacher reports that "because of Kenneth's low mentality his progress is slow, but it is steady." She and Mrs. Hunt both think that the boy is speaking more distinctly.

CASE 91. HENRY WILD   SIX YEARS AND SIX MONTHS
Temper tantrums. Destructive. Quarrels with other children.
Progressive brain lesion.

Home Situation.—Henry is an illegitimate child who has spent his life in many hospitals and orphanages. Nothing is known of his paternal relatives. His mother is suspected of being feeble-minded.

Developmental History.—Henry's development has been unusually slow. He was late in talking and walking. Even now he can walk but a few steps at a time without falling. He sleeps and eats well and is fairly well nourished. There is evidence of a progressive brain lesion and the three intelligence tests which he has taken in the last year and a half have given successive IQs of 75, 69 and 65.

History of Adjustments.—The characteristics which Henry now shows have been a gradual development. He is very affectionate and at the same time sensitive. His temper is rather marked and he is destructive and throws things around when he is angry. He plays only with younger children and quarrels frequently with them, particularly when they cross him.

Suggested Treatment.—Henry must be cared for in an institution.

CASE 92. AARON SORENSON   SIX YEARS AND SIX MONTHS
Feeding problem. Speech problem. Twitches. Shy. Dislikes school.
Feeling of inferiority. Constitutionally inferior physically.
Over-solicitous mother.

Home Situation.—The Sorenson home is happy and congenial. Mr. Sorenson drives a milk wagon in his own name, is a very easy-going man who never scolds and never "takes it out" on his wife and children when he is tired. He is home a good part of the afternoon and he and Aaron are "great pals." Sometimes in vacation he takes the boy around the milk route with him and he tries consistently to have Aaron confide in him. Mr. Sorenson seems to be of average intelligence and anxious to do what he can for the welfare of his children. Mrs. Sorenson worries more than her husband. She admits that she spoils Aaron, saying that the others don't understand him as well as she does. The other children are a brother of nineteen, a sister of seventeen who has a cleft palate, a sister of twelve said to be a "tomboy, husky and wild," and a sister of ten who is "more refined" than the others. Neither parent exacts immediate response to commands.

Developmental History.—Aaron is said to have been a well baby though he cried most of his first year. He did not walk until he was two and even then he did not have good motor control. He was generally slow in developing and seemed to be a quiet, phlegmatic child. He was talking a little by the age of three but he does not speak distinctly yet and has recently begun to stutter. He has a slightly defective gait and walks with his feet turned out. He has had no contagious diseases except measles. At present Aaron is average height and weight for his age, but looks frail and colorless. His tonsils are moderately large, the arch of his palate is high and narrow and he is tongue-tied. There is much jerking of the head, body, and extremities. On the intelligence test he received an IQ of 90 and in this his attention shifted rapidly.

History of Adjustments.—Various physicians have said that Aaron was feebleminded, but the parents have been dissatisfied with this diagnosis. He fatigues easily, especially when playing with other children. He twitches in his sleep somewhat as he twitches when walking, but he appears to sleep well. He is finicky about eating. He dislikes all vegetables except potatoes and his mother has never forced him to eat anything he dislikes, but tries, on the contrary, to provide the food of which he is fond. He soiled his clothes until he was four but there has been no recent history of soiling clothes or of enuresis.

Aaron was sent to kindergarten at the age of five and a half but he has never liked it. At first he seemed shy of adults and cried a great deal. It seemed almost impossible for him to sit still and concentrate on anything. He had a great deal of difficulty in speaking and frequently failed to make himself understood. At such times he becomes very angry and begins to stutter. In addition to his indistinct enunciation, Aaron talks baby-talk but he has improved so much since entering a speech class that none of the teachers are sure that mental deficiency is the cause of his difficulty. They feel, rather, that if the speech defect were corrected he would probably progress in school.

Aaron likes to play by himself and will be content indefinitely with his blocks. When playing with other children 'he wants his own way and they generally give in to him. He fights back when they start fighting with him. His brothers and sisters sometimes tease him and he then becomes angry and cries. At times Aaron is very irritable and Mrs. Sorenson has found the best treatment of this to be undressing him and putting him to bed for a time or letting him go upstairs for a rest. He recovers from the crossness quite easily. Aaron is generally cheerful and good natured, especially on those days when he does not seem so nervous. He is not afraid of anything but he is sensitive. His mother thinks he felt badly about not being promoted in school. He is shy with strangers and not particularly affectionate. From babyhood he has disliked being touched and spanking seems to make him angry. In the clinic it was evident that Mrs. Sorenson was oversolicitous and she was continually prompting him. His reactions were rather infantile. It was difficult to encourage him to talk. When he could not say "six" in answer to a question he held up the proper number of fingers instead.

Suggested Treatment.—Aaron seems to be consitutionally inferior physically. His evident feeling of inferiority on account of his speech defect puts him at a disadvantage in a new or strange situation, and this makes him restless. A specialist should be consulted about an operation on Aaron's tongue. If possible he should be sent to a private school where he can receive special attention in speech and habit training. Mrs. Sorenson should train him as much as possible in habits of self-help and self-reliance. He should be allowed to work for brief periods only and should take many brief rests.

CASE 93. RALPH THAXTER   SIX YEARS AND NINE MONTHS

Bedwetting. Mischievous. Selfish. Stubborn. Nervous. Destructive. Swears. Disharmony in the home. Inconsistent discipline.

Home Conditions.—Mr. Thaxter is a street-car motor-man. He has always been of a melancholy and nervous temperament.

He is quick tempered, uses profane and vile language when angry and at these times beats the children severely. He lisps and has a foreign accent. Mr. Thaxter's early married life was unhappy and he started drinking heavily. When his wife died, however, he stopped. He soon married again because he "wanted a home for his children." His first wife was a nervous, flighty woman who displayed frequent temper tantrums and neglected the children. The second wife was a widow, who married Mr. Thaxter for the sake of a "home for her own children and because she was sorry for his children." She feels that this second marriage was "beneath her." She speaks in a loud voice and often says the children "will drive her to distraction." Besides the father, the step-mother, and Ralph there are in the family a step-sister, age nine who is slow in school, a step-brother age six, an own sister age eight said to be bright and active, a brother age seven, and a sister age five.

Developmental History.—Ralph was an active and healthy baby but he had at least two fainting spells when he was about nine months old. In these spells "his eyes rolled and he lost consciousness for a few minutes" but he "came to after having a little water sprinkled on his head and he was sick only a few hours." He learned to walk and talk at about ten months. Except for influenza at the age of two and an occasional ear-ache he has had no diseases. At the present time he is well developed and nourished. On the intelligence test he received an IQ of 108. Here he was often very slow in answering because of too great absorption in some other topic. He is left-handed.

History of Adjustments.—Ralph's mother died when he was two and after that for a time he was moved from one boarding home to another, never remaining in any one longer than a couple of months. When his father remarried, Ralph and the other children were reassembled.

Ralph has always had a good appetite and he eats whatever is put before him. In fact, when he was living in a boarding home which failed to provide enough food, Ralph acquired the habit of visiting the neighbor's garbage cans for food to supplement his meals. He now sleeps quietly though for a period when he was three he cried out frequently in the night that dogs were after him. Enuresis has been no problem at school, but at home for a long time was persistent both night and day. Three years ago his step-mother tried to cure it by putting Ralph in a tub of cold water, by making him wash his own clothes, and by tying him naked to the bed-post and having the other children shame him. But none of these methods were effective and the enuresis continued until a few months ago when a neighbor offered the boy ten cents for every week in which enuresis did not occur. This method worked like a charm.

Ralph was sent to kindergarten at the age of five and a half and is now in grade 1-A. He is bright and enthusiastic about his work, restless and mischievous, but not a behavior problem. The other children like him and he often leads them in games. When disciplined he is apt to cry quickly. Ralph appears to be growing somewhat more fidgety of late. He is very careless about his clothes. The step-mother starts him off whole and clean every morning, but by the time he arrives at school Ralph is ragged and dirty. He is selfish, denies all blame and shifts the responsibility of misdeeds onto others. He is stubborn, boisterous, talkative and "nervous." He fears punishment, but after being punished he turns around and does the same thing over again. Mr. Thaxter says Ralph "can't tell the truth unless he forgets himself." He is destructive and likes to pick apart even the few playthings with which he is provided. He has never been known to run away and he responds well to praise. Ralph uses profane language.

The step-mother is evidently inconsistent. She sometimes complains because the father does not punish the children and the next day complains that he is brutal. Mr. Thaxter, in turn, complains that every night the step-mother would have the children lined up against the wall for him to punish when he came in. Six months ago Mrs. Thaxter threatened to leave as she "didn't wish to sacrifice her life any longer." The father then applied to a charitable organization to place his children since he felt that would be the only solution to his domestic troubles. This quarrel blew over and the family are all still living together.

Suggested Treatment.—The chief trouble here seems to lie in an unsatisfactory home life, disharmony between the parents aggravated by economic pressure. Ralph has had inconsistent discipline, frequent changes in control, and unstable supervision. No provisions have been made for his interests and recreation. A capable, imaginative and sensitive boy like Ralph should not be forced to live with a step-mother like Mrs. Thaxter. He should be placed in a foster home.

Later History.—Mr. Thaxter reports after seven months that during the six months that Ralph has been living in a boarding home he has been quite happy and well behaved.

CASE 94. RUBY KNIGHT   SIX YEARS AND NINE MONTHS
    No particular problem. Poor heredity. Poor environment.

Home Conditions.—There has been considerable instability in both sides of Ruby's family. Her maternal grandfather deserted his family when the children were small, and her father is an easygoing, lazy semi-skilled laborer, called by a neighbor "poor white trash." He has never worked steadily and lately has not seemed "quite bright." As a result of helping a brother-in-law carry off stolen goods, Mr. Knight is now serving a sentence in a reformatory. Mrs. Knight is a silent, rather morose woman who has never made friends easily. She seems disinterested in keeping her house and her children clean, is discouraged and does not try to improve the home conditions. The family have moved around a great deal and are now living in dirty ramshackle rooms. Mrs. Knight doesn't even bother to make over clothes that are given to her for the children. She merely pins the things up sufficiently to let the child walk without tumbling down, and lets it go. When the father is home he is very good natured, takes no part in punishment and lets the children do as they please. Mrs. Knight usually punishes by spanking. Ruby has a brother age nineteen in the navy, a sister seventeen, whose husband gets arrested frequently for one offense or another, a sister of fifteen, a sister fourteen, a sister thirteen, a brother eleven, and a sister of eight at home.

Developmental History.—Ruby was not a fussy baby as far as her mother can remember. She walked at nine months and talked at about a year. She had chicken pox at four and measles at five. At present she is slightly under-weight and under-nourished, and has several carious teeth. Her IQ is 99.

History of Adjustments.—Ruby is an example of a child with poor heredity and poor environment showing no behavior problems. She sleeps well and is not fussy about her food. She is active and fond of being out of doors, and does not like to help about the house. Ruby is ready to attempt any task suggested but tends to give up easily. She is active, cheerful, easy-going and enjoys almost everything. She is stubborn at times, but generally obedient. She gets along well with other children and is truthful and honest. Her speech is rather indistinct. Ruby was sent to kindergarten at five, and is now in first grade. The teacher reports that she learns easily and seems quite bright.

CASE 95. LUELLA ANDREWS   SIX YEARS AND TEN MONTHS
    (see case 70)

CASE 96. EARL VAUGHN   SIX YEARS AND TEN MONTHS
            Feminine characteristics. Solitary.

Home Situation.—The Vaughns live on a farm in a sparsely settled district. Mr. Vaughn is rather a nonentity, neither liked or disliked by the other farmers of the settlement. Mrs. Vaughn is a rather high-strung woman who is anxious to be in the limelight. She longs to be a leader and frequently starts clubs and "movements" but all her projects end shortly in quarrels. Earl has two older brothers, one aged twenty is a keen student who has worked his way through high school in a nearby town and is now endeavoring to earn money enough to go to college. He is considered rather peculiar by the other young persons of his own age for he prefers books to people. He and Earl have much in common temperamentally and are quite companionable in spite of the great discrepancy in their ages. The other brother is fourteen, no student, interested in the farm and very popular socially. Mrs. Vaughn has always been very anxious to have a daughter and when Earl arrived she made no effort to conceal her disappointment. She bemoaned the fact that all the lace and ruffles and crocheting which she had prepared would be "lost on a boy."

Developmental History.—Earl was an ordinarily good baby and except for chicken pox at three has never been ill. His present physical condition is good. He walked at about eighteen months. His speech is not clear even yet, for he lisps, uses baby-talk, and displays oral inactivity. His IQ is 100.

History of Adjustments.—When Earl was about two years old, Mrs. Vaughn noticed that he was extremely modest, and refused to be accompanied to the toilet by any one except his mother. As she considered this a desirable trait, no effort was made to modify Earl's behavior. Neither did she attempt to persuade him to play with more masculine toys when he seemed to prefer dolls, ironing-boards, little dishes, and the like. In fact Mrs. Vaughn seemed pleased to have such a "little lady" for a son. When he was three she decided that the time had come when she must give up her baby and dress him in boy's clothes so she provided little Russian blouse suits and attempted to cut his curls. She was highly amused, and apparently secretly pleased when Earl utterly refused to part with his curls and would not wear the suits until he was allowed to wear a starched, and lace-ruffled petticoat underneath the blouse. Not until the last year has it been possible, according to the mother, to dress the child wholly in boy's clothing. His curls were cut off at the age of five.

Earl has been a solitary child, partly because there has been no child nearby except a girl cousin who was a tomboy, and partly because his frail little grandmother who lives on the next farm has encouraged him to spend considerable time puttering around her garden with her. He never runs or climbs and is excessively distressed if any of his clothing gets torn or soiled. Earl is very fond of going to Sunday School though he does not like his day school so well. There the other children pick on him, laugh at his pronunciation and his girlish ways.

Mrs. Vaughn apparently realizes that his feminine traits are likely to be a drawback in his later life and she has made half-hearted attempts to change them, but she evidently derives considerable emotional satisfaction from his likeness to the desired daughter.

CASE 97. OLAF AMUNDSEN   SIX YEARS AND TEN MONTHS
School problem. Sensitive. Starts fires.

Home Situation.—The Amundsens live in a pleasant house in a good neighborhood. Mr. Amundsen is a quiet man who speaks slowly and is rather uncommunicative. He is said to be stern, though reasonable and slow to anger. He is a travelling salesman and is usually away from home except for Saturdays and Sundays and so does not see much of his children. Olaf's mother was a quiet, refined woman. Her death a year ago is thought to have been the result of the shock she received some months earlier when Olaf's arm was nearly cut off. The family at present consists of the father, a maternal aunt, a nine year old brother, Olaf and his twin sister. Neither the twin nor the older brother is a problem. Mr. Amundsen very evidently prefers these other children and he and the aunt seem to feel that Olaf is responsible for his mother's death, since the accident to his arm was due to the child's own carelessness.

Developmental History.—At birth Olaf was thought to be dead. He was revived but remained delicate for several weeks. This aroused a permanent pity for him in his mother. He walked at eighteen months and talked at two years. Since infancy he has been exceptionally healthy and has had no diseases except chicken pox. He has, however, due to his own carelessness had several accidents. His arm was nearly cut off by a truck, he burned himself by sitting on a hot stove, and he has cut his hands and legs several times. He can stand a great deal of physical suffering. At present he is large for his age and fairly well nourished. His posture is poor, his gait is peculiar, and he looks pale and anaemic. He has poor and irregular teeth. On the intelligence test Olaf received an IQ of 105.

History of Adjustments.—Olaf has an enormous appetite and has never been a feeding problem. He is defiant of authority and is definitely antagonistic toward his father though he rather fears him. He can be bribed with money, but seldom commanded. He forgets punishment as soon as it is administered and the only effective discipline is putting him to bed. He hates to be still. Olaf is jealous of his brother and recently tore a new blouse of his beyond repair. To his twin sister, however, he is devoted, sits gazing at her and shares everything with her. The boy has initiative, is frank, truthful, and likeable. He is very sensitive and feels that his father is unjust in his partiality for the other children. He probably misses the affection of his mother. Olaf plays constantly with his hands or some object.

Most of his mischievous conduct occurs when he is with other boys. He has started fires in closets at home several times, set fire to his mother's bedspread once, and once to a nearby garage. No particulars are known about the circumstances. Olaf is not at all impressed with the danger, though he has been shown fire-ruins. Last winter he stuffed some mail boxes full of snow. He was with other boys at the time, but is thought to have been the leader. Olaf's own explanation is that he did not know it was wrong. He explains the fires by saying "I like to see the blaze" and he apparently sets them to gain attention.

When Olaf first went to kindergarten just before he was six he drooled, but with constant reminding he corrected this. Three months later he entered first grade and has progressed steadily. He is now in second grade. His work is mediocre and he is never ashamed of failing. The teacher thinks he is intelligent but inattentive. Although the other children like him, they are annoyed by his constant whispering and throwing scraps of paper in their desks, and so on.

Suggested Treatment.—Mr. Amundsen must change his attitude and be more of a companion. Olaf should be allowed to tend the fire in the furnace and should have fire works. He should, if possible, be placed in a new room at school to start fresh and one where his twin sister is not, for he adores her too much now. He should be supplied with occupations which interest him.

Later History.—Two months later Olaf is reported as happier, not so jealous, showing rare outbursts of temper and setting no more fires. His father refuses to separate him and his sister at school.

CASE 98. LOUISE WHEELWRIGHT SIX YEARS AND ELEVEN MONTHS
Fears. Jealous. Handles genitals. "Mean" to siblings. Hard to manage.
Father possibly psychopathic.

Home Situation.—Both sides of Louise's family have had contacts with charitable organizations for many years. Mr. Wheelwright, himself, was confined in a reform school when he was sixteen and has been in the work-house for drunkenness and for neglecting his family. He was considered insane by the neighbors. In fits of anger he frequently kicked the children, broke up the furniture and deliberately attempted to choke his wife. Although himself immoral, he was intensely jealous of his wife and refused to allow her to leave the house alone. He could seldom hold a job for more than a few days at a time on account of his drinking and he has often been unable to pay the rent or to provide sufficient food to keep the children from hunger. The family have moved from shack to shack and from city to city. Three years ago Mr. Wheelwright deserted the family altogether and two years later his wife secured a divorce. Mrs. Wheelwright appears to be a simple-minded, weak-willed woman who is easily influenced and overpowered by stronger individuals. Since her husband's desertion she has worked out as a laundress and she and the children have lived in one boarding house after another. The woman with whom they board at present seems sincerely interested in the children and fond of them. She does not allow them to play with other children in the neighborhood for fear of contagious diseases. Louise has a four year old sister and a three year old brother who get along well with each other.

Developmental History.—Louise was a well and happy baby. She walked at eleven months and talked at thirteen months. She had no early illnesses except a light attack of influenza at three months and mumps at five years. At present she is well developed though somewhat underweight. She has dark circles under her eyes and looks tired. Her thyroid is slightly enlarged and she has a blowing systolic heart murmur at the apex. Her IQ is 109.

History of Adjustments.—Louise sleeps quietly and has a fairly good appetite. She has never sucked her thumb or shown any particular fears. The boarding mother claims that the child has acquired an abnormal amount of sex information though at the clinic she gave no evidence of this and the physician concluded that the boarding mother was misinterpreting a slight tendency to handle the sex organs.

Mrs. Wheelwright acknowledges that Louise is helpful around the house but both mother and grandmother think she is "just like her father, with a violent temper, talking mean to her mother, stamping her feet, and being in general hard to manage." They claim she is extremely jealous of any attention to her sister and brother. She is very "mean" to them. When told not to touch her sister's sore finger, she hit it with a stick. She has also been known to scratch her brother. Louise apparently has never treated any other children as she does her own brother and sister.

Six months ago, Louise was sent to first grade. At first she was very timid, even actually fearful. The teacher was sorry for her and so was especially kind. Louise soon responded to the teacher's affection and developed into a "sweet, lovable child." She is no problem in school, does good work and plays happily with the other children.

Suggested Treatment.—Louise has evidently never been subjected to a consistent habit training program and her activities have been too greatly circumscribed. Mrs. Wheelwright gave considerable evidence of a psychopathic condition in herself when she talked to the physician. She sooner or later contradicted every statement she made and she told of dizzy and "staggering" spells. She is probably taking out on Louise her hatred of her husband, on the basis that the child resembles him. Louise needs an examination for thyroid and heart trouble, needs special help in school, a building up of her physical condition, habit training, and a disciplinary regime.

CASE 99.   WILLARD WILCOX   SIX YEARS AND ELEVEN MONTHS
Selfconscious. Thumbsucking. Petty stealing. School problem.

Home Situation.—Mr. Wilcox is said to have been "rather wild and reckless as a boy" but has lately expressed a regret that his father hadn't kept him in school instead of buying him a car.

He is a big, strong man who is apparently lazy both physically and mentally. He lets his wife run the furnace while he lounges around reading the paper. He has been out of work frequently during the last seven or eight years. He lacks experience and training and has no ambitions for work higher than that of a day laborer. He takes little interest in the children and knows little about them. He does not disagree with his wife on discipline; he simply lets her do it all. Mrs. Wilcox is quite different from her husband. She taught in a secondary school before her marriage, and for the last few years has been clerking in a near-by store during rush hours. She is energetic, ambitious and very fond of her family. She seems to use wise methods in controlling the children. When corporal punishment is necessary she administers it promptly, and when she gives orders the children know they must obey. Willard's five year old brother is a handsome child, showing none of the undesirable traits which Willard developed soon after entering school. The family live in a meagrely furnished upper flat in a rather undesirable neighborhood.

Developmental History.—As a baby Willard presented no particular difficulties. He walked at fourteen months and talked soon after he was a year old. He had a light case of chicken pox at six and broke his collar bone the same year. At present he shows an average development and nutrition. There are some dental caries and possibly near-sightedness since he holds all reading materials very near even when the print is large. He has an IQ of 111. He gave some evidence of color-blindness and is evidently left-handed although he has been trained to use his right hand. His reading ability is not up to his general level of ability.

History of Adjustments.—Willard is a friendly little boy who meets strangers with his dimples in evidence and a twinkle in his eye. He occasionally shows a slight stutter and he apparently tries to conceal his self-consciousness by an ostentatious "smartness" of speech and action. Mrs. Wilcox says that the boy sleeps quietly though he wakens to go to the toilet several times each night. All his life he has slept with his thumbs in his mouth in spite of his mother's putting unpleasant liquids on them, tying up his hands, and so on. He never sucks his thumbs in the daytime and he has never bitten his nails. Willard is lovable and affectionate at home and enjoys helping his mother with the housework though he likes to argue and to be coaxed first.

Willard was sent to kindergarten when he was five and a half and is now in grade 1-A. His attendance at school is very irregular. He loiters on the way and is often tardy. Last fall it was occasionally necessary to send a school police boy to search for him when he didn't report. At these times Willard was usually found playing near a fire engine house. In school the boy fails to pay attention or to concentrate. His seat is in a back corner of a room containing forty children and Willard finds watching things outside the window or watching the other children in the room far more interesting than applying himself to his school work. When the teacher calls on him to read she often can not tell whether the boy is actually reading the print or is reciting from memory. He does much better work in a small group where the teacher can give the children individual attention. The other children do not like Willard because of his boldness and unrepressed activity. With them he is aggressive and demands his own way. He pouts and whines when the teacher refuses what he wants, but she tries to ignore him. He has no respect for the boy police at school and will walk out of line and talk when expected to be silent. He does not hold a grudge when punished though the punishments seem to have little effect. Several times Willard has appropriated toys which the other children have brought to school and has taken them home, but he has shown no serious tendencies in this direction.

Suggested Treatment.—Willard should be given a seat in the front of the school-room. He should be allowed to use his left hand if he prefers it. He should be coached on reading. Mrs. Wilcox should take Willard for a careful eye examination and for dental treatment.

Later History.—Three months later Willard is reported as doing good work in grade 2-B, is showing much more interest, paying closer attention, and is much more agreeable. He now has an honor position in the marching lines for good behavior. He has been to see an oculist and has been given glasses. Two months later the teacher reported that she now finds Willard an "interesting and attractive" child. He uses his left hand at the blackboard, and his right hand for desk work.

Case 100. OLIVER NELSON   Six Years and Eleven Months

Fatigue. Feeding problem. Bedwetting. Fidgety. Unhappy. Listless. Forgetful. School problem. Cries easily.

Home Situation.—The family situation of the Nelsons is one that would be expected to result in all sorts of serious behavior difficulties and delinquencies, and this case is interesting chiefly because it shows that there are rather unintelligent mothers who nevertheless are able to handle a difficult situation extremely well.

The family background is poor. There is the history of a maternal uncle who while in prison for highway robbery tried to escape and was shot by a guard. There is the history of the mother, a beautiful girl who resented the burden of a family and housework, became increasingly discontented during the years of her married life, was nagging and irritable, attempted suicide and finally died of pneumonia a few days after the birth of her youngest child. There is the history of a father who was backward in school and now is able barely to support his family. He appears to help his wife in her efforts with the children but does not himself carry out any active program in the household. He spends practically all of Sunday in church and so does not see the children even then. He gives his entire pay envelope to his wife and never questions her apportionment of the money. There is the history of a step-mother of probably rather limited mentality with two illegitimate children, a term in a reform school, and marriage with Mr. Nelson three days after she came to keep house for him. She is strong, healthy, and good natured with unbounded energy. She is very fond of all the children though she sees their faults. There is the history of the mixture of "his children, her children, and their children" which might be expected to produce trouble. And there is the history of the mother of the first wife as a source of perpetual conflict in the home. She is very devout and has been extremely alarmed for fear the second wife was attempting to alienate her grandchildren from her church. She has spread reports of Mrs. Nelson's malicious neglect of her step-children and partiality toward her own, has reported her to the police and to various humane societies as abusing the children, and has done everything in her power to prejudice her grandchildren against their step-mother. After this had gone on some time and several agents had been to the house only to find the children well treated, Mr. Nelson determined to interfere. Since then the grandmother has withdrawn and now fortunately has nothing to do with the family.

The children of the family are as follows: Children of the first wife, Sam, age eight, who is no problem but is "just like a little old man toward the younger children." He is rather nervous and fidgety, and bites his nails. His IQ is 102. Then Oliver whom we will discuss later. Then Leo, age five with an IQ of 52. His mother died a few days after his birth and he was placed in an orphanage. There he developed rickets and was in such an undernourished state that death was predicted at the time his father remarried and took him home. He is still extremely rachitic. The step-mother thinks he is improving rapidly physically, but she is discouraged by his inability to care for himself. He is listless and apparently has no control of the sphincters. The step-mother's own children are a girl age eight, healthy and well developed with an IQ of 96; and another girl age five now in kindergarten. The other group of children, those of Mr. Nelson by his second wife are a girl of two, bright, healthy and self-reliant and the constant companion of Leo, and a tiny baby girl, healthy and well developed and the pet of the entire family. This large family live in a neat and clean (but somewhat over-crowded) house on the outskirts of the city. The family are more or less ostracized by the neighbors but the children seem quite happy and contented with each other as playmates.

Oliver appears to have been very much attached to his own mother and his grandmother purposely increased this feeling in him and prejudiced him against the step-mother, but after he had known the step-mother for several months and found that she was uniformly kind and affectionate toward him, he changed and is now devoted to her. Oliver, as well as each of the other children in the family, has his own household tasks and if any one child fails to do his share, another is asked to do it in his place. There is no mention of punishment or reprimand but the child who has fulfilled the duty of the other never fails to remind the mother that the miscreant is not to have his cake or goody for Sunday night supper. Mrs. Nelson says this is the only form of discipline that she uses and that she never has to be harsh with any of the children.

Developmental History.—Little is known of Oliver's early development. He is now under developed, has an unusually large head and is a mouth breather. He has had measles, whooping cough, scarlet fever, chicken pox, and scabies. His tonsils were removed this last year. He has frequent and rather violent nosebleeds. He is physically inferior with a high and narrow palate. He has an IQ of 83.

History of Adjustments.—Oliver shows a number of difficulties but not nearly as many and not nearly as serious ones as we might expect. He fatigues easily. He has always been a feeding problem though he is showing considerable improvement with consistent training. He refuses some vegetables and revolts at soup. He craves sweets. He still wets the bed. Oliver is very fidgety, rather morose and unhappy. He sits with an expressionless gaze. His father becomes annoyed by his listlessness and prods him to "smile a bit and cheer up." Any such criticism is usually met by tears. He is forgetful when his mother sends him on errands and she is uncertain whether this is due to a poor memory or to the nervous excitement of going to the store. He is willing and helpful around the house.

At the age of five Oliver was sent to kindergarten and the next year promoted to grade one. He is now repeating 1-B. In the clinic he was shy at first with no spontaneous conversation, but apparently not blocked or repressed.

Suggested Treatment.—Oliver needs general physical building up and possibly cod liver oil.

Later History.—A year later Oliver is now in grade 1-A after spending three terms in 1-B. He is neat and clean but his mother has been having difficulty in making him brush his teeth. After another year we have the report that Oliver is repeating grade 2-B and is having great difficulty with reading. The other children call him a dumb-bell. The child seems somewhat depressed as a result of the school failures and the antagonistic attitude of the neighborhood around the home. The clinic then advised an eye examination (which was negative), special coaching in reading, a speech class and if possible a change of neighborhood for the entire family. Two months later Oliver is in grade 2-A and under the special coaching his reading has improved considerably.

INDEX

The figures in black face refer to case numbers, and the figures in Roman type refer to the page. Thus, in first entry, Ach, Herbert, the reference is to case **6** which will be found on page 32.

Cases **1** to **17** are two year olds; cases **18** to **33** are three year olds; cases **34** to **57** are four year olds; cases **58** to **75** are five year olds; and cases **76** to **100** are six year olds.